T0146468

STANDING TALL

HOW A MAN CAN PROTECT HIS FAMILY

STANDING
TALL

STEVE
FARRAR

Multnomah Publishers® *Sisters, Oregon*

STANDING TALL
published by Multnomah Publishers, Inc.

© 1994, 2001 by Steve Farrar

International Standard Book Number: 978-1-59052-867-9

Cover image by Tony Stone Images

Scripture quotations are from:
New American Standard Bible
© 1960, 1977 by the Lockman Foundation
The Holy Bible, New International Version (NIV)
© 1973, 1984 by International Bible Society,
used by permission of Zondervan Publishing House

Multnomah is a trademark of Multnomah Publishers, Inc.,
and is registered in the U.S. Patent and Trademark Office.

The colophon is a trademark of Multnomah Publishers, Inc.

ALL RIGHTS RESERVED
No part of this publication may be reproduced, stored in a retrieval system,
or transmitted, in any form or by any means—electronic, mechanical,
photocopying, recording, or otherwise—without prior written permission.

For information:
MULTNOMAH PUBLISHERS, INC. • 601 N. LARCH ST. • SISTERS, OR 97759

Library of Congress Cataloging-in-Publication Data:

Farrar, Steve.
    Standing tall / Steve Farrar.
        p. cm.
    ISBN 0-88070-618-X
    ISBN 1-57673-788-8
    ISBN 978-1-59052-867-9
    1. Fathers—Religious life. 2. United States—History—
Religious aspects—Christianity. 3. United States—Moral conditions.
4. United states—Social conditions—1980- 5. Farrar, Steve.
I. Title.
    BV4846.F384 1994
    248.8'421—dc20
                                                            94-136
                                                            CIP

146651086

To Mary

For over twenty-five years we have ridden
the river of life together.
There have been times when we
lashed ourselves together
because the rapids and white water
were severe and rocky.
And then there were those
sections of water where
together we savored
the placid stillness
and gazed upon the dazzling beauty
that surrounded us.
We have navigated rough waters,
and we have enjoyed calm waters,
and there will be more of each ahead.
That's just the way the Lord
has designed His rivers.
Smooth and quiet one minute,
wild and treacherous the next.
But that's okay.
We're in this canoe together.
And never has a man enjoyed
the ride more than I.

CONTENTS

Acknowledgments 9

Introduction 11

1. Ridin' for the Brand 13

2. The Whites of Their Eyes 31

3. Dads Who Draw the Line 47

4. When America Lynched Common Sense 67

5. Showdown in Samaria 91

6. High Noon for a Nation
   Gay Wrongs, Part 1 109

7. When the House Begins to Fall
   Gay Wrongs, Part 2 123

8. Elijah Stands Tall 147

9. Fighting the Good Fight 165

10. Seven Ways to Help Your Kids Stand Tall 183

11. Womenfolk 201

12. Outposts of Civilization 211

Notes 225

ACKNOWLEDGMENTS

It has been said that if you see a turtle sitting on a fence post, it's for sure he had some help getting up there. The same could be said for me. I had a tremendous amount of help getting here from some very gifted and dedicated compatriots.

- Larry Libby is an editor with a unique combination of abilities. Editorially speaking, Larry threw some key blocks for me when I was hemmed in on the sideline. That's why Larry has my vote for All-Pro. I can't tell you how glad I am that we're playing on the same team.

- Don Jacobson and Eric Weber are key players in the excellent publishing team known as Multnomah. Many thanks to them for their professionalism and their desire to speak truth. These are men who, when they make a promise, keep a promise. It's a genuine pleasure to be in the harness with them.

- Stu Weber, Gary Rosberg, Andy McQuitty, Jim Litchfield, Steve Lawson, and my wife, Mary, all took their valuable time to evaluate the manuscript and make insightful comments and suggestions. Their encouragement especially fueled this project when we were nearing the finish line.

- Bob and Judy Brown graciously allowed me to hide out in the canyon at a time when solitude was needed and necessary. A week without a ringing phone is worth at least a pound of gold. And so are good friends.

- James Hall designed a great cover for the book, and David Uttley came up with the title. Thanks, guys.

- John Bethany, Mike Miller, Deedee Smith, and Mike Wolverton are a staff sent from heaven. They covered a multitude of bases at the office when I was both preoccupied and occupied with this book. Thanks, guys, for a job well done.

INTRODUCTION

I don't smoke cigarettes or rob banks. But I do write books. And believe me, *any* of these activities can kill you.

In the classic Hollywood western *Butch Cassidy and the Sundance Kid,* the two wily outlaws find themselves hemmed in by an angry posse. Completely outflanked by rifle-toting deputies, they are backed up against the edge of a hundred-foot cliff. Looking over the precipice behind them, they see a raging, frothy river clawing its way through the canyon far below.

Butch suggests they jump.

Sundance refuses. Butch won't give up the idea and Sundance continues to resist. Finally, with the lawmen closing in for the kill, Butch asks in desperation why Sundance won't jump. Meekly, Sundance admits that he can't swim.

Butch laughs and then utters these immortal words: "You can't swim? Shoot, the *fall* will probably kill you anyway!"

With that, they both step off the cliff.

This book has just about done me in. I knew it might, back when I stepped off the cliff four months ago. Here's the problem: The stuff I am writing about is heavy stuff. Every man in America who loves his family should be aware of these issues, but…taking them on is no Sunday picnic. These are intense, gut-wrenching questions that can consume huge hunks of emotional energy.

As you read the pages that follow, you'll see just what I mean. Some of these issues will probably make you angry, frustrated, and tense. And frankly, they *need* to upset you. If you're not upset when you finish some of these chapters, then I haven't done a good job.

But the purpose of this book is not to kill you. The purpose of this book is to help men wise up to some conditions that threaten not only our children, but our very existence as a nation.

Yes, there are some pretty heavy chapters. These chapters talk about the overwhelming need for male leadership in families across America. I'll be trying to divulge the enemy's strategies to utterly destroy the once-strong pillars of biblical morality on which this nation was founded.

But as I said, I'm not writing just to raise men's blood pressure. I don't want to send any guys packing because of hypertension or coronary arrest. For that reason, there are other chapters that will remind us that God is in charge, that He is working His plan, and that He will take care of us as we seek to take care of our families.

In other words, these pages have some warning, some encouragement, and some hands-on help for standing tall in a culture that wants Christian men to check out of any significant involvement in the destiny of our nation.

I have carried the message of this book in my heart for several years now. I am convinced that it is a message the enemy does not want you to hear. For if you hear the message, then you will be motivated to square your shoulders, step up to the line, and fight for your family, perhaps as never before. And the *last* thing the enemy wants is for God's men to be charged up and ready to take on the very gates of hell.

But that's exactly what we have to do, gentlemen.

Because the gates of hell have set up shop just outside our front doors. The gates of hell cast their shadows onto our schools, the media, the movies, the TV sitcoms, and the morals of our nation.

Enough is enough. It's time to stand tall.

So if you're with me, let's take a flying leap over the edge.

It should be quite a ride.

1

RIDIN' FOR THE BRAND

Unprincipled men and women,
disdainful of their moral heritage and skeptical of Truth itself,
are destroying our civilization by weakening
the very pillars upon which it rests.
CHARLES COLSON

The Brand.

Every man and boy in the Old West knew the importance of a brand. A brand was the mark that a rancher would burn on his stock.

But it was more than that. Much more.

When a man hooked up with a certain outfit, it was said that he was "ridin' for the brand." Louis L'Amour, the great storyteller of the American West, etches out for us the significance of those four potent words:

The term "riding for the brand" was an expression of loyalty to a man's employer or the particular outfit he rode for. It was considered a compliment of the highest order in an almost feudal society. If a man did not like a ranch or the way they conducted their affairs he was free to quit, and many did, but if he stayed on he gave loyalty and expected it.

A man was rarely judged by his past, only by his actions. Many a man who came west left things behind him he would rather forget, so it was not the custom to ask questions. Much was forgiven if a man had courage and integrity and if he did his job. If a man gave less than his best, somebody always had to take up the slack, and he was not admired.[1]

This is a book for men. Men who are ridin' for the brand. To be more specific, it's written to men who are not their own. The reason they are not their own is simple. They've been bought with a price.

Every man I know who is ridin' for the brand has things in his past he wishes he could go back and undo. But that really isn't necessary. Once you've been called to ride for the brand, your past is taken care of. Totally and completely. Because you've been bought with a price. And the blood that bought you covers it all. Your past, your present, and your future.

What is this brand? Let me suggest that it's the Two-One-Two brand. The Two-One-Two is very direct and to the point. It signifies two nail scars in His hands, one spear in His side, and two more nail scars in His feet. That's why we're not our own, and that's the price He paid. For you. For me. We're ridin' for the brand.

Ridin' for the brand is a high calling. No, that's not quite right. It is the *highest* calling. It's the brand that is above every other brand and every other name. For it signifies the name of the Lord Jesus Christ. When a man begins to understand the privilege and responsibility of owning this brand, he will give it nothing less than his best. A man who is ridin' for the brand is not judged by his past, but he is expected to have courage, integrity, and to do his job.

What is that job? What are the duties of a man who rides for the brand? That question deserves a definitive answer. And there's no better place to start than with some other guys, in another time, in another place. Why would we start with them? Simple. They were ridin' for the brand.

GUMLESS WARRIORS

When you buy a Bible, it usually doesn't come with a stick of bubble gum. The only thing I remember that comes with a stick of bubble gum is a pack of baseball cards. But that's exactly why every Bible should come with bubble gum. For every Bible contains 1 Chronicles 11 and 12. Those two chapters are a set of baseball cards. Well, not baseball cards. *Warrior* cards.

When I was a kid, I had hundreds of baseball and football cards. Back in the fifties, it was not unusual for me to invest my allowance in complete sets of the American and National Leagues in baseball, plus the NFL. Each of those cards had a picture of the player on the front. On the back, it had a brief biography, a few important stats, and one or two of the player's most outstanding achievements. I know a lot of guys who still collect baseball cards, football cards, basketball cards, and even *hockey* cards, for crying out loud.

But I don't know anyone with a set of warrior cards. That's why we need 1 Chronicles 11 and 12. These stirring Old Testament chapters are the equivalent of going down to the drugstore, laying down your money, and collecting a package of cards with a stick of bubble gum. This section in Chronicles doesn't come with pictures, but it does have brief biographies, a few stats, and some of the more outstanding achievements of a group of guys known across the territory as David's Mighty Men.

God's men have never been strangers to battle. In the days of King David, God's men were often fighting physical battles. That's part of riding for the brand. Today, in our culture, God's men are fighting spiritual battles. That's also riding for the brand. The stakes are high. For two very sacred and fundamental components of our lives are under attack from our culture.

What are these two sacred factors that we are sworn to defend?

They are our faith and our families.

That's why we are going to battle. In our culture, a man who is riding for the brand is going to have to stand tall against his enemies. And at some point, he's going to have to fight. There's no getting around it.

ONWARD CHRISTIAN SOLDIERS

David was a gifted man. He was a poet, a musician, and a king. But above everything else, David was a warrior. David was no stranger to war or bloodshed.

That's why you should know David well. You may not be a poet, a musician, or a king, but if you are a Christian husband and father, you are a warrior.

You see, over time, a man who is riding for the brand will be called by different names. In one culture it's "warrior," in another it might be "cowboy," in another, "conquistador." But it's really the same thing. It's just another way of describing a man who is riding for the brand.

David was a commander and a leader. That kind of warrior always draws other men to his cause. David had some spectacular warriors in his army. They were so remarkable that Scripture reports not only their names, but also their exploits.

You've probably never heard of these guys. But if you'd been around in David's day, you would have recognized them immediately. They were known men. Guys such as Ahiezer, the head of the tribe of Benjamin. Ahiezer's warriors were respected and feared throughout that chunk of the world. Men such as Joash, the two brothers Jeziel and Pelet, Beracah, Jehu the Anathothite, and Ishmaiah the Gibeonite.

Tough men. Dangerous men. Men who were absolutely fearless.

These were the men who came to David at Ziklag, while he was banished from the presence of Saul son of Kish (they were among the warriors who helped him in battle; they were armed with bows and were able to shoot arrows or to sling stones right-handed or left-handed). (1 Chronicles 12:1–2, NIV)

Did you notice that these guys were switch-hitters? That was very important for a warrior back then, for if you were wounded in your right arm and you were a natural right-hander, then you were probably dead meat. But these guys had thought of that possibility. I wonder how many hundreds, if not thousands, of hours they spent working with slings and swords with their natural hand and their unnatural hand. So if they were wounded in one shoulder, no problem. They'd just switch hands, suck it up, and keep fighting.

As good as these men were, David had others just as good. The same account in 1 Chronicles 12 also records the exploits of the Gadites (v. 8). The Gadites were a company of crack troops who just showed up one day at David's door. The son of Jesse looked outside one morning and—bang!—

there they were. That was the interesting thing about David's army. None of these men were drafted; they were all volunteers. They believed in David and they believed in his cause. They wanted to back David's star and ride in David's posse. The young general from Judah must have been mighty glad to see them.

Scripture describes them this way:

They were brave warriors, ready for battle and able to handle the shield and spear. Their faces were the faces of lions, and they were as swift as gazelles in the mountains. (1 Chronicles 12:8, NIV)

These guys were not only tough, but they were also *fast.* Speed has always been important in warfare, and the men from Gad had it. They were fierce and they were quick. Their chief was Ezer, but also mentioned by name are Obadiah, the second in command, Eliab the third, Mishmannah the fourth, Jeremiah the fifth, Attai the sixth, Eliel the seventh, Johanan the eighth, Elzabad the ninth, Jeremiah the tenth, and Machbannai the eleventh. The reason they are referred to this way is that they were each commanders. Here are their stats: "These Gadites were army commanders; the least was a match for a hundred, and the greatest for a thousand" (1 Chronicles 12:14, NIV).

These guys could handle themselves. They were sort of David's Navy SEALs. Verse 15 records that they were the ones "who crossed the Jordan in the first month when it was overflowing all its banks, and they put to flight everyone living in the valleys, to the east and to the west" (NIV).

The first month was flood season, and when the Jordan flooded, it was serious stuff. You're talking about getting across a raging, fast-moving torrent of water a mile wide and 150 feet deep. That's no exaggeration. In other words, these guys weren't swimming laps at the YMCA. The Gadites were the original iron men. A triathlon would have been a piece of cake to the boys from Gad.

Why were they willing to make such a dangerous crossing at such a treacherous time of year? They wanted to ride for the brand.

First Chronicles 12 goes on to list a number of other warriors who joined David when he was at a place called Hebron. All of these men were clear-eyed, battle-hardened soldiers. The best Israel had to offer. They were the top riders, the Special Forces, the Green Berets of the nation. They were David's Doomsday Defense. They are listed by tribe, and in some cases by exploit, as the men of Zebulun, who are described as "experienced soldiers prepared for battle with every type of weapon" (v. 33, NIV).

MVWs (MOST VALUABLE WARRIORS)

In the midst of this all-star lineup of warriors in 1 Chronicles 12 is a reference to a group of men who were absolutely unique to any army that has ever been gathered. These men were not listed by their names. Only their tribe is mentioned. They are not described as warriors who could fight with either hand or swim across the Jordan at flood stage.

So who were they, and what could they do?

They were the "men of Issachar, *who understood the times and knew what Israel should do*" (v. 32, NIV, emphasis mine).

Now don't get me wrong. The men of Issachar could fight, or they wouldn't have been listed with the others. These guys could hold their own against anyone. But they had another dimension to them, and quite frankly it was a dimension the others apparently didn't have. David desperately needed their contribution, and so did the entire nation. These men understood the times, and as a result, they knew what Israel should do.

In other words, these men had two things that made them a cut above the rest:

- The men of Issachar had discernment.
- The men of Issachar had direction.

The men of Issachar saw what others didn't see. They looked behind the physical events and circumstances and realized there were spiritual forces influencing the conditions and situations of the nation from behind a parted curtain. That's why the men of Issachar were so valuable for warfare. They had discernment. They could stare a hole right through the obvious and see what wasn't obvious. Because of their discernment, they were then able to offer direction. Direction that was accurate and on target.

The men of Issachar were worth their weight in gold because they understood the times. Because they understood their culture and the forces at work behind the scenes, they knew what Israel should do.

As I read through 1 Chronicles 11 and 12, I was impressed by the thousands of men from each tribe who were listed in David's army. Thousands upon thousands. Yet when it came to the men of Issachar, it mentions only their two hundred chiefs. These men appear to be the cream of the crop. There weren't twenty thousand of them; there were just two hundred. Yet their influence left its mark on all the rest.

They had discernment.

All of David's mighty men rode for the brand. But the men of Issachar saw what the other men didn't see, perceived what the other men didn't perceive.

As a result, they knew what needed to be done.

Gentlemen, we are living in a culture that is changing so fast it's hard to assimilate the changes. And the changes are not for the good. America is deteriorating morally and spiritually at an alarming rate. There are spiritual forces behind those changes. If you are going to function effectively as the spiritual leader of your home, you must be able to discern what is happening in this culture. You must do for your family what the men of Issachar did for Israel.

You must understand the times.

And if you understand the times, then you will know what your family should do.

This book is an attempt to help us understand our times. For—in the sovereignty of God—these are the very times when a lot of us happen to be raising our families. Our children are living in a culture that is light-years away from the culture in which we were raised. You might be raising your family in the same town where you grew up. Your kids might even go to the same schools you attended. You might drive on the same streets where you used to ride your bike as a kid. On the surface, it may look pretty much the same.

But that's an illusion.

The streets may be the same, the schools may be the same, the neighborhoods may be the same, but the town is a different town than it was thirty years ago because at least two things have changed.

- The thinking has changed.
- The values have changed.

Because the thinking has changed and the values have changed, our outlook for the future has changed.

Peggy Noonan writes a profoundly accurate picture of where many of us baby boomers are:

> I don't know many people [our age] who don't have a sense that they were born into a healthier country, and that they have seen the culture deteriorate before their eyes....
>
> You don't have to look far for the fraying of the social fabric. Crime, the schools, the courts. Watch Channel 35 in New York and see your culture. See men and women, homo- and hetero-, dressed in black leather, masturbating each other and simulating sadomasochistic ritual. Realize this is pumped into everyone's living room, including your own, where your eight-year-old is flipping channels. Then talk to a pollster. You too will declare you are pessimistic about your country's future; you too will say we are on the wrong track.[2]

The America we remember from our youth and the America in which we are raising our kids are so different it's almost as if they're two different countries. In a sense, they are different countries. Today's America is being ripped apart by forces our parents and grandparents would never have dreamed of. It is the clash of these forces that is becoming known in our day as the "cultural war."

THE CULTURAL WAR

The cultural war is a reality. But what is it? Tom Bethell has done as good a job as anyone in giving a summary of the cultural war:

> The "culture" really refers to a widely held set of beliefs about the purpose of life and the way in which society should be organized as a consequence. Those beliefs, in the U.S. as in the West generally, were for a long time broadly Judeo-Christian. Those who did not share these underlying religious beliefs were nonetheless for the most part willing to assent to them, and to accept the resulting framework of law and custom: abortion is wrong and should be illegal, homosexual

behavior is shameful and should be frowned on, at best closeted; sexual intercourse should await matrimony and thereafter be confined to one's spouse.

All those beliefs have for a long time been under attack and have now been very widely discarded. Laws have been changed to reflect the new "reality." The results of abandoning the old culture are now apparent in the gay bathhouses and the AIDS wards, in the addiction treatment centers, in the crumbling inner cities, in the street gangs of the underclass, in the abortion clinics, in the high-school clinics that distribute condoms and Norplant, in the welfare offices, in the public housing projects, in the crime and illegitimacy rates, and most recently in the activities of the serial killer from Michigan, Jack Kevorkian.[3]

If any more evidence is really necessary to prove that America has changed, William Bennett can provide it. Bennett, the former secretary of education, first published his *Index of Leading Cultural Indicators* in the mid-1990s. The astonishing results demonstrated just how great the changes in this country have been since the early 1960s. I suggest that you read this next paragraph slowly and thoughtfully.

[During this] same 30 year period there has been a 560 percent increase in violent crime; more than a 400 percent increase in illegitimate births; a quadrupling in divorce rates; a tripling of the percentage of children living in single-parent homes; more than a 200 percent increase in the teenage suicide rate, and a drop of almost 80 points in the S.A.T. scores.[4]

Bennett has proven our suspicions. This country has changed. We are being defeated, not by some outside threat, but by our own choices. We are hemorrhaging internally, and if the bleeding isn't stopped, this nation will not survive.

Is there any doubt that America has changed? The statistics prove it, our eyes behold it, and sometimes, friends, our minds simply can't believe it. America has changed as a nation, and we have changed from the inside.

When I was a kid, there was a great rush in this country to build bomb shelters. Everyone knew that the Soviet Union had the ability to rain missiles down just about anywhere in our country. Who would have believed back then that what would ultimately bring America down was not the Russians, but *ourselves*.

Paul Harvey illustrates the point by telling a rather gruesome story. It's a story about hunting. More precisely, it's a story that describes the process an Eskimo uses to hunt down a wolf.

> First, the Eskimo coats his knife blade with animal blood and allows it to freeze. Then he adds another layer of blood, and another, until the blade is completely concealed by frozen blood.
>
> Next, the hunter fixes his knife in the ground with the blade up. When a wolf follows his sensitive nose to the source of the scent and discovers the bait, he licks it, tasting the fresh frozen blood. He begins to lick faster, more and more vigorously, lapping the blade until the keen edge is bare. Feverishly now, harder and harder the wolf licks the blade in the Arctic night. So great becomes his cravings for blood that the wolf does not notice the razor-sharp sting of the naked blade on his own tongue, nor does he recognize the instant at which his insatiable thirst is being satisfied by his own warm blood. His carnivorous appetite just craves more—until the dawn finds him dead in the snow.[5]

A cagey wolf might have thought his greatest enemy was man. Not so. His greatest enemy was himself. The wolf was destroyed by internal lust. The real threat was not from the outside; it was from the inside. As it was with the wolf so it is with America. For there are forces at work within this country that are as insidious as any that can ever come from the outside. It is these forces that day by day are eroding the moral infrastructure of this great land.

I believe it was Pogo who said, "We have seen the enemy, and he is us."

THE LOWEST COMMON DENOMINATOR

When I read Bennett's report of the decline of the nation, I found it difficult to assimilate all of the information. Quite frankly, I was overwhelmed not only by the statistics, but also by the complexity and scope of our social and moral deterioration. It quickly became apparent that I was going to have to reduce all of those statistics to their lowest common denominator.

You remember the "lowest common denominator," don't you? It's the single most important principle to successfully working fractions. It is also very effective in working *fractures*. Fractured children, fractured families, and fractured nations.

I believe that if you look at every major pressing social issue in this country, whether it's teenage pregnancy, child abuse, drive-by shootings, teenage suicide, or the divorce rate, and reduce each of those problems to its lowest common denominator, you will find in each case the same root cause.

That cause is a lack of male leadership.

With every major social problem in America, somewhere and in some way a father has failed to give leadership to his family. That's the root cause of every pressing social issue in this country. The deterioration of our culture has accelerated dramatically because fathers who are willing to lead are in the minority. And that's the lowest common denominator. Daniel Patrick Moynihan observed this fact in 1965:

> From the wild Irish slums of the nineteenth century Eastern seaboard to the riot-torn suburbs of Los Angeles, there is one unmistakable lesson in American history: a community that allows a large number of young men (and women) to grow up in broken families, dominated by women, never acquiring any stable relationship to male authority, never acquiring any set of rational expectations about the future…that community asks for and gets chaos.[6]

Chaos.

That word accurately describes what is coming in our country because of the breakdown of male leadership. When authority breaks down, first in the home and then, consequently, in the nation, chaos is the inevitable and frightening result.

We are closer to chaos than one might want to believe. When authority breaks down and the consequences of breaking authority cease to exist, then you can be assured that we, as a nation, are well on our way to chaos. You've heard the phrase "Crime doesn't pay." The truth of the matter is that in this culture of ours, those who abuse and despise authority are paid very well indeed.

Senator Phil Gramm wrote a piece for the *New York Times* where he cited a study from Texas A&M that calculated the amount of time that a person committing a crime in 1990—the last year complete statistics were available—could reasonably expect to spend in prison. The conclusions were shocking. On average,

- a person committing murder can expect to spend 1.8 years in prison;
- a person committing rape can expect sixty days;
- a person committing robbery will serve an average prison time of twenty-three days;
- a person convicted of arson can expect 6.7 days;
- a person committing aggravated assault averages 6.4 days;
- a person stealing a car can reasonably expect to spend a day and a half in jail.[7]

With the breakdown of authority that begins in our homes and spreads to our schools and courts, it becomes clear that crime does pay. And it pays very well. America is quickly becoming a country that is sending a message to scores of young people, and the message is this:

- authority is not important;
- you can willfully break authority (although we would prefer that you don't);
- if you choose to break authority and punishment cannot be avoided, we will make it as easy on you as we possibly can.

It has been a time-honored tradition in New York City for kids to try to open fire hydrants on hot summer days to cool off. The fire department would then come along and close the hydrants so that the water pressure could be kept up. Columnist John Leo reports that this "game" has been getting ugly.

Now, the kids open the hydrants and if they are pugnacious about it, the firefighters back down and the kids win. In certain areas, rocks and bottles are tossed whenever hydrant closers arrive. The standard practice of offering free spray caps hasn't worked. In one case, a hard spray was aimed at the cab of a fire truck, causing it to crash. It's not just about access to water during a heat wave. There's a sense that turf is somehow being invaded by the fire department and that the firefighters are authority figures worth rebelling against.

So the fire department issued a new directive. Now firefighters are under orders to back off from confrontations, though they are allowed to try closing the hydrants "at a later time." (Perhaps in the fall?)

In effect the city has "solved" its problem by turning control of the hydrants over to potential troublemakers. On the street, everyone now knows that firefighters will fade away even if growled at. A letter to the editor of New York's *Daily News* correctly called it a scary precedent that borders on anarchy. What's next, the letter writer asked, police avoiding gun-bearing thugs?

Policies such as these are as demoralizing as major crimes. Cities are haunted by the fear that no one is really in charge, that the nominal government can't or won't keep order, that it will cede any ground and collapse any standard to avoid trouble. Authorities keep backpedaling. Menaces aren't confronted. They are adjusted to and become part of the system.[8]

In this story about kids playing with fire hydrants, the lowest common denominator is the absence of male leadership. Thirty years ago, if a kid was fooling around with a fire hydrant and then spoke disrespectfully to a fireman, his father would have taken down the strap and given him a few well-placed licks on his rear end. Today, there is no father present in the home, and if he were there, and if he did take down his strap, some bureaucrats would have his rear end in jail for damaging the psyche of his son.

We need to get something straight. Ridin' for the brand means that a man leads his family. That's part of the high calling. It's such a necessary part that the Scriptures clearly teach that a man who doesn't lead his family and control his children is unfit for leadership in the church. Why would family leadership be a prerequisite for a man who is called to serve as leader in his church?

Ridin' for the brand means that you are a man who is salt and light. A society cannot survive without male leadership. For when male leadership ceases to be a reality in the home, we are only one generation away from anarchy in the streets. This is the direction that our nation is going. If we lose male leadership in Christian families, then this country is finished for sure.

Ridin' for the brand means that a man is not a follower. He stands tall. He is a leader. And that's the name of the game, gentlemen. It's leadership.

If you are a leader instead of a follower, or if up to now you have been a follower but have a *desire* to be a leader of your family, then I think I can make you a promise. This book will make you a more effective husband and a more effective father, because it will enable you to discern more accurately the forces that are actively at work in our nation to bring down everything that you value and love.

But if a man doesn't understand what the forces and issues are, how can he give effective leadership to his family? How can he give direction to his children? How can he prepare them for what they are going to face if he doesn't know what they are going to face?

Our children are facing and will face moral challenges that were absolutely unthinkable when we were growing up. That's why we must familiarize ourselves with the forces that are at work to destroy the innocence of our children in this culture.

These forces are serious. Deadly serious.

That's why we have to be like the sons of Issachar.

The men of Issachar had vision, and we must have vision.

Soon after the completion of Disney World, someone said, "Isn't it a shame Walt Disney didn't live to see this?"

Mike Vance, creative director of Disney Studios, replied, "He *did* see it. That's why it's here."

This is a book for men. It's a book on how to lead your family in the midst of a culture hostile to Christian principles. It is designed to help you discern, and it is designed to help you give direction. Quite frankly, it's a follow-up to *Point Man*, a book I wrote to men a few years ago on how to lead a family spiritually.

If you are a husband and father, then you are leading your family through the moral chaos of this culture. You are the point man. There is an enemy who is very real, and he has a plan to pick you off and neutralize you from leading your family. When you are the point man, to a great degree the very survival of your family depends upon the caliber of your leadership.

The book that you hold in your hands is designed to familiarize you with the changing spiritual influences that we are fighting against. Battles change with time, and this battle is no different. We need to see clearly what we are up against.

There is nothing worse than a blind point man. Helen Keller was once asked if there was anything worse than being blind. "Yes, there is," she replied. "It is having sight but no vision."

Let me be honest with you. I am genuinely amazed at how many blind Christian men I run into. Now don't get me wrong. They have physical vision. They might even be twenty-twenty when it comes to seeing stuff on the surface. What they are missing is *spiritual vision*. They don't have spiritual discernment. They don't understand the times, and most tragically, when it comes to spiritual matters, they don't have a clue as to what their families should do.

I see it in the choices they make. I see it in the lack of direction they give to their children. I see it when Christian fathers allow their children to attend objectionable movies. A man of discernment would never allow his children to attend certain movies. A man without vision thinks to himself, *It's just a movie.* A man of vision knows that it's more than a movie. It's a carefully crafted and marketed piece of propaganda promoting a value system contrary to everything right, just, godly, and good.

But the man without vision doesn't see that. So he hands his ten-year-old a ticket and throws him to a pack of rabidly immoral, Hollywood-bred pit bulls.

That's like a guy who is leading a patrol through enemy-occupied territory and notices a trip wire partially exposed in the underbrush, just off the dimly marked path. If he thinks to himself, *It's just a wire,* he will soon be headed home in either a helicopter or a body bag. A man giving leadership to a patrol or a family must have eyes to see and understand what isn't apparent on the surface.

A man with vision is a man of discernment.

And what is discernment?

Discernment is looking at the same thing as everyone else and seeing something very different. You see the inevitable implications that will come from what appears to be just an isolated situation. A man who can't see with discernment is not an effective husband or father. He has to see the bigger picture. He has to have vision. He must be a man of action.

In Lewis Carroll's *Alice in Wonderland,* there is a particular dialogue between Alice and the Cheshire Cat in which Alice inquires of the cat, "Would you tell me, please, which way I ought to go from here?"

"That depends a good deal on where you want to get to," the Cat replies.

"I don't much care where," says Alice.

"Then it doesn't matter," returns the Cat, "which way you go."

You wouldn't be reading this book if you didn't care where your family was going. You care, and you care deeply. That's precisely why you need vision to discern this culture in which you are raising your family. Men who ride for the brand are men of vision. They understand the times, and they know what their families should do.

How much vision do we need?

Just enough to see the barbarians.

WALKING TALL

1. Read 1 Chronicles 11:15–19 and 12:16–18. Describe the character of the loyalty of these men to David and to the Lord. What can we as men learn from these displays of unflinching, unintimidated loyalty to the cause?

2. Review 1 Chronicles 12:32. In view of the conditions in America today, how can we be more like the sons of Issachar?

3. Look at 1 Chronicles 12:33. What might the biblical writer have had in mind when he described the men of Zebulun as men of "undivided heart"? What kinds of influences in our contemporary culture might give Christian men a *divided* heart? What will it take for us to ride for the brand like those guys from Zebulun?

4. Note the last words in 1 Chronicles 12: "There was joy in Israel." What do you see in the preceding verses of the chapter, particularly in verses 38 through 40, that might have brought such joy? What clues does the writer leave that might make us more joyful men today—even in a country where Christian values are being trashed?

5. Take a moment to look up Proverbs 29:18. If you have copies of the New International Version, the New American Standard Version, and the King James Version, check out the differences in wording. Solomon seems to be equating "vision," with prophetic vision or divine revelation. In other words, the Scriptures! What evidence in today's culture do you see of Solomon's warning about those who remove such "vision" from a nation or people?

2

THE WHITES
OF THEIR EYES

At what point, then, is the approach of danger to be expected?
I answer, if it ever reaches us it must spring up amongst us;
it cannot come from abroad.
ABRAHAM LINCOLN

I live in Texas. There are still a lot of cowboys wherever you go in Texas. Whether it's San Antonio, El Paso, Tyler, or Dallas, you'll see cowboys everywhere. And the telltale sign of a genuine Texas cowboy is his Stetson.

All over Texas you'll run into men wearing their Stetsons. Texas is full of cowboys and cowboy hats. You will also see a lot of pickups. And that explains something that you might not know if you live outside Texas. Do you know why cowboys always roll up the brims of their Stetsons on the sides? It's so three of them can fit in the cab of a pickup.

Attila the Hun didn't wear a Stetson, and he didn't drive a pickup. But he was as wild as any cowboy who ever rode in Texas. Attila the Hun was a barbarian. The words *Hun* and *barbarian* go hand in hand. Wess Roberts describes the men who followed Attila's leadership:

Individually, the Huns were a spirited, perfidious [I don't know what perfidious means, but it sure sounds good] people without common purpose other than to establish their next campsite. Commodities for internal trade didn't exist, so they sought out villages to lay waste to in order to obtain booty that would later be used as barter for food and other supplies necessary for their survival....

Clad in the skins and the furs of beasts, many of the Huns were characterized by somber, yellowish skin, long arms, large chests, and narrow, slanted eyes with a dull glitter of mingled cunning and cruelty. Their warriors had skulls deformed in childhood by a wooden apparatus held fast by leather tongs. The scant beards of the warriors were the result of their cheeks having been seared with hot irons in their youth to retard the growth of facial hair.

They ate raw meat toughened by having been carried in pouches between their thighs or between the flanks of their horses. A portion of their nutrition came from drinking mare's milk.

The weapons of the horde were considered unsophisticated and outlandish even in their own time. Their spirit as warriors was driven by a lust for rapid and sustained movement in pursuit of a paradise of glory filled with pillage and booty.

To the civilized world they were barbarians not far removed from wild animals in both appearance and lifestyle. The mere presence of the horde often instilled sufficient terror in the people of the region that they abandoned their villages without resistance or subsequent reprisal.[9]

CHOOSING SIDES

The Green Bay Packers were the team of the sixties, the Pittsburgh Steelers the team of the seventies, and the San Francisco 49ers owned the eighties. The Dallas Cowboys won the most Super Bowls in the nineties. Which team would you choose over the others? That's a tough call.

There are some who would pick Attila and the Huns as the greatest warriors in history. Others would take Alexander the Great and his crew. Personally, I'll stick with David and his Mighty Men. I'll stack them up against a bunch of wild-eyed barbarians anytime. For David's men had Someone on their side that no other nation in history can claim in the same way. His name is Yahweh, the Creator and Ruler of all things.

Why did God give David such a group of mighty warriors? David had his Mighty Men because Israel needed such men to protect them from the barbarian hordes that surrounded them on every side. David and all of Israel were encircled by barbarians.

By the way—so are we.

The only difference is that the barbarians in our culture don't *look like* barbarians. That's precisely why you need discernment. Without discernment, you won't be able to recognize the barbarians.

Charles Colson delivers this sobering diagnosis:

> I believe that we do face a crisis in Western culture, and that it presents the greatest threat to civilization since the barbarians invaded Rome. I believe that today in the West, and particularly in America, the new barbarians are all around us. We have bred them in our families and trained them in our classrooms. They inhabit our legislatures, our courts, our film studios, and our churches. Most of them are attractive and pleasant; their ideas are persuasive and subtle. Yet these men and women threaten our most cherished institutions and our very character as a people.... Today's barbarians are ladies and gentlemen. Yet behind their pleasant, civilized veneer lurks an unpleasant intolerance that threatens the very processes of pluralism and freedom they claim to defend.[10]

I recently came across one of these new barbarians in one of my children's school. I got so close that I could see the whites of his eyes. As a matter of fact, I had to go toe-to-toe with him in front of two hundred people.

The last thing he looked like was a barbarian. Truthfully, he was a well-dressed, very pleasant-looking gentleman in his early forties. He certainly did not look threatening. He looked like a nice, average American who might live across the street from you. He was married and had two children. He was a nice guy, with a nice job, with a nice family, from a nice neighborhood.

He was also a barbarian.

In our state in the last decade, Planned Parenthood and its philosophical cohorts have made several attempts to mandate sex education courses in public schools, beginning with kindergarten. These people believe that five-year-olds should be given information that will help them determine their "sexual orientation." That is nothing short of criminal.

A few years ago in Texas, a new bill was introduced that was very, very vague. It was vague by design. In previous attempts to pass mandated sex education that would take the control from the local school boards, the Planned Parenthood proposals were soundly defeated. So Planned Parenthood decided to be delightfully nonspecific. Concerned parents in our community called several meetings about the new proposal. One was called by a group of mothers who opposed the bill. I made sure that I attended that one. Another was called two weeks later by some people who were for the bill. I decided I had better show up at that one as well.

When I arrived for the meeting, things had already gotten underway. There were close to two hundred parents in the cafeteria. The sponsors made it very clear that the meeting was not sponsored by the school district. Rather, it was being called by a man in our community who was concerned that the previous meeting had been too conservative and one-sided. He had invited an official from Planned Parenthood to debate the issues with a lady who represented the other side.

Because I got to the meeting late, I was unaware of the arrangements. The lady "representing the conservative side" was so inarticulate and noncommittal that I thought throughout the evening that she, too, was representing the side of Planned Parenthood.

It wasn't much of a debate.

Basically, the guy from Planned Parenthood spent two hours giving half-truths, inaccurate statistics, and evasive responses to written questions. The man who had called the meeting announced that no questions would be taken from the floor. All questions were to be written. The moderator read through the questions and submitted the ones he thought the guest should answer. That's called censorship.

After about forty-five minutes of watching the moderator lob the Planned Parenthood representative nice, easy, and mostly irrelevant questions, a man to my left spoke from the floor. He was told that questions weren't being taken from the floor. He replied that *his* question was not being addressed, and he went directly into his question. It was a very good question. He had obviously done his homework, and the man from Planned Parenthood hemmed and hawed but could not give a definitive response. For the first time, someone had called his bluff. He wasn't looking very sharp as he took the first "unscreened" question from the floor.

That's when I decided to speak up.

The moderator reminded me that questions were not being taken from the floor. I replied that my question was germane to the discussion and was being ignored. So I went ahead and asked my question.

"Sir, two years ago a group known as APPAC (Adolescent Pregnancy and Parenthood Advisory Council) made some recommendations to the state legislature encouraging the passing of a mandatory sex education curriculum."

"Yes," replied the man. "I was a part of that committee."

"In your recommendations you advised the state to adopt a curriculum that included a 'bill of rights' for adolescents. I am quoting from the bill of rights that you encouraged the state to adopt."

I then read a section of the document that said that every adolescent has a "right" to "confidential reproductive health care services."

"Sir, as I understand this 'right' that you feel that young children should have, it means that my daughter could walk into one of your clinics at school, be given advice and encouragement that is contrary to the moral values that my wife and I have taught, and I would never know about it. She could also be given a birth control device without my knowledge. Why is it that you believe that your counselors have a moral viewpoint superior to ours—and why is it that your counselors should have access to my child in such a way that undercuts my parental authority?"

A murmur rippled through the audience.

The Planned Parenthood spokesman then began a lengthy and evasive response that appealed to some Supreme Court decision on the question of "privacy." As he continued his verbal gymnastics he made a reference that was very innocuous and harmless on the surface.

That's when I jumped in again.

"Sir, by that reference, aren't you referring to abortion?"

The room suddenly got very quiet because I had said the "A" word.

His reply was nothing short of phenomenal.

"I was not referring to abortion. *Planned Parenthood has nothing to do with abortion.*"

I couldn't believe my ears. I looked around and saw a few others shaking their heads in disbelief. The tragedy was that a number of people in the room believed him. After all, he was such a nice guy with such a nice family.

"Sir," I said, "you are deliberately misstating the truth."

Immediately some people began to boo and hiss at me. Others started to applaud.

"I am not. Planned Parenthood has nothing to do with abortion. I'm the director and I ought to know."

"That is exactly right, sir. You should know and you *do* know, and I know. You are deliberately attempting to persuade this audience of something that is not true."

The booing got louder, and the hisses became more pronounced. A woman turned around right in front of me and declared that she found my remarks offensive. I smiled at her and kept going.

The guest speaker was now backtracking by citing another Supreme Court decision. I responded by reminding him that the Supreme Court, in its Dred Scott decision, had ruled that black people were nothing but chattel. In other words, the Supreme Court could be very, very wrong.

It was getting late, and the meeting was hastily brought to a conclusion. It was then that the man from Planned Parenthood walked up to me.

"So you think I lied to this audience tonight?"

"Sir," I replied, "I know that you did. And so do you."

He proceeded to explain to me that "technically" they did not directly perform abortions in their office. However, they did underwrite the budgets of twenty-some abortion clinics in several counties. He then detailed other activities they supported that directly encouraged and funded abortions.

"Sir, why didn't you say all of this up in front of the audience? You deliberately withheld this information—and you did it in order to leave an impression that was blatantly untrue."

"Well," he replied, "I must say that I am deeply disturbed by the hatred, fear tactics, and half-truths being spread by the other side!"

"So what you are doing bothers you, right?"

He looked at me completely confused. "Of course not! I was referring to the other side!"

"Oh," I responded. "After watching your performance this evening, I was sure that you were referring to yourself." I then smiled and said, "It's nothing personal." In my mind I thought, *It's just that you want my children. And that's not going to happen.*

I don't enjoy people booing and hissing at me. But do you know why I spoke up? I spoke up because I'm riding for the brand. To have *not* spoken up would have been nothing less than a betrayal of the Lord Jesus Christ. I guarantee that *He* would have spoken up because the lives of little children are at stake. In my opinion, that's something worth standing up for.

You see, gentlemen, because we are surrounded by these new barbarians, it means that Christian husbands and fathers are going to have to do three things. A man who is going to ride for the brand and fight the good fight must (along with his wife):

- discern his culture;
- defend his convictions;
- disciple his children.

That's it. That's the abbreviated job description of a point man in this culture. That's what it's going to take to battle the barbarians. That's what it's going to take to stand tall and defend your family.

I took the time to recount my experience to you because it demonstrates in microcosm the real issue going on in this country. What was it about this nicely dressed gentleman that was so barbaric? It was what he believed. You see, this man believes in something called *moral relativism.* I believe in *moral absolutes.* And so do you. I seriously doubt that you would be reading this if you didn't believe in moral absolutes. It used to be that the vast majority of Americans believed in moral absolutes, but that is no longer the case. As Pat Buchanan observed, "Americans of left and right no longer share the same religion, the same values, the same codes of morality; we only inhabit the same piece of land."

SAMPLE THE EXAMPLE

In case it is still unclear as to what we mean when we refer to moral absolutes, allow me to offer the following examples:

- "I am the LORD your God, who brought you out of the land of Egypt, out of the house of slavery. You shall have no other gods before Me."
- "You shall not make for yourself an idol, or any likeness of what is in heaven above or on the earth beneath or in the water under the earth. You shall not worship them or serve them; for I, the LORD your God, am a jealous God, visiting the iniquity of the fathers on the children, on the third and fourth generations of those who hate Me, but showing lovingkindness to thousands, to those who love Me and keep my commandments."
- "You shall not take the name of the LORD your God in vain, for the LORD will not leave him unpunished who takes His name in vain."
- "Remember the sabbath day, to keep it holy."
- "Honor your father and your mother, that your days may be prolonged in the land which the LORD your God gives you."
- "You shall not murder."
- "You shall not commit adultery."
- "You shall not steal."
- "You shall not bear false witness against your neighbor."
- "You shall not covet your neighbor's house; you shall not covet your neighbor's wife."

These examples of moral absolutes are brought to you through the courtesy of Moses and Western civilization as founded on the Word of God as recorded in Exodus 20:2–17. For hundreds and hundreds of years, anyone who did not believe these particular moral absolutes was considered, quite frankly, a barbarian.

THE BARBARIAN COAST

Why is moral relativism so barbaric? It is barbaric because of what it believes. Here's the bottom line. A person who believes in moral relativism basically believes in two things:

- There is no absolute truth;
- Therefore, everything is permitted.

Moral relativism took off in this country in the sixties. A case could be made that the first capital of moral relativism was the Haight-Ashbury district of San Francisco. San Francisco was once known as the Barbary Coast; what it gave birth to in the sixties was nothing less than the Barbarian Coast of free love, free speech, and moral relativism.

This was the thinking behind the cultural shift that took place in America right around 1968. It was taught in our universities and spread like wildfire through the collective consciousness of students all over America. But those students of the sixties are no longer students. They are the opinion-shapers of our society—professors, members of Congress, judges, school board members. What they believe is that there is no absolute truth; therefore, everything is permitted.

In the sixties it was called "doing your own thing." If you bought into moral relativism in the sixties, you could let your hair grow, sleep around, smoke dope, and basically do whatever you wanted. That's what it looked like on the surface. But underneath, it was even more terrifying. In Colson's words, moral relativism means that:

> In every decision a person stands alone. Because there are no moral absolutes, there are no value-associated reasons to make one decision over another. We may as readily choose to ignore a neighbor rather than help him, to cheat rather than be honest, to kill rather than let live...the outcome of our choices carries no moral weight.
>
> No longer are we guided by virtue or tradition. Selfish passions breed freely.... Gone are any notions of duty to our fellow man and to the Creator. As a result, there is no straight edge of truth by which to measure one's life. Truth is pliable and relative; it can take whatever shape we want.[11]

Gentlemen, we are raising our kids in this sewer of moral relativism. If your kids buy into this philosophy, it will ruin their lives. Here's the deal, guys. Our kids won't know anything else unless they see it in our lives. Our kids won't know that there are moral absolutes unless they absolutely see those truths *lived out* in our lives.

In thirty years moral relativism has swept through our culture with blinding speed and pervasiveness. It's everywhere. Our kids read it in the newspapers and magazines, watch it on TV, hear it on the talk shows, listen to it on CDs and cassettes, and are taught it in the majority of public schools.

You see, when I was a kid the Ten Commandments were posted in our classroom. As a result, every kid in my public school classroom knew that it was wrong to steal, wrong to cheat, wrong to murder, and wrong to lie. Why did we know that? Because almighty God said so. It was God who had given that moral code to Moses on Sinai.

But today our kids are growing up in a culture where someone will say, "Well, that may be wrong for *you,* but that doesn't mean it's wrong for *me.*" That is moral relativism.

The point is this, gentlemen: We can't rely on the culture to back up what we are trying to teach to our children. That's the way it was in the fifties, when I was growing up. Generally speaking, the culture was going to back up the values that my parents were trying to teach me. That's why Ozzie didn't leave Harriet, David, and Ricky and run off with some sweet young thing he met at the office. (Did Ozzie ever go into the office?) The culture and the media upheld and sustained the moral absolutes of the Ten Commandments, therefore it was unthinkable for Ozzie to commit adultery. But those days are gone.

We have now completely lost our moral compass in this country. In modern America, bad is good and good is bad. Listen to the network anchors, listen to the Oprahs and Rosies, listen to the godless messages of the TV sitcoms, listen to the messages written on the editorial pages of the nation's newspapers. They are all saying that on the moral compass south is north and north is south.

They are wrong.

Almighty God determined the magnetic fields that cause compasses to point north, and He wrote the moral law that gives civilized people equilibrium and balance. And He has revoked neither the magnetic fields nor His moral law.

North is still north.

South is still south.

Homosexuality is still perversion.

Abortion is still the taking of innocent human life.

Yet the media is working in a concerted effort with the other elitists to give the impression that its distorted morality is the "consensus" of this country. It uses the power of vicious sarcasm and slanted reporting to shout down anyone who would stand up to its twisted and convoluted morality. Its primary weapon is sheer intimidation. Saying that there is such a thing as absolute truth is the very thing that moral relativism detests and despises.

THE WAY WE WERE

Allan Bloom knew American culture. Liberals viciously attacked his book *The Closing of the American Mind* when it was released. Bloom, who recently passed away, was a liberal Jewish scholar greatly respected in academic circles. At least he was until he wrote his critique of American higher education. Bloom describes what has happened to the average American family as a result of moral relativism:

> Parents do not have the legal or moral authority they had in the Old World. They lack self-confidence as educators of their children, generously believing that they will be better than their parents, not only in well-being, but in moral, bodily, and intellectual virtue. There is always a more or less open belief in progress, while the past appears poor and contemptible. The future, which is open-ended, cannot be prescribed to by parents, and it eclipses the past which they know to be inferior....
>
> Parents can no longer control the atmosphere of the home and have even lost the will to do so. With great subtlety and energy, television enters not only the room, but also the tastes of old and young alike, appealing to the immediately pleasant and subverting whatever does not conform to it. Nietzsche said that the newspaper had replaced prayer in the life of the modern bourgeois, meaning that the busy, the cheap, the ephemeral, had usurped all that remained of the eternal in his daily life. Now television has replaced the newspaper.[12]

Today television is perhaps the primary spokesman for moral relativism. Approximately one hundred years prior to the 1950s, philosopher Soren Kierkegaard wrote: "Suppose someone invented an instrument, a convenient little talking tube which, say, could be heard over the whole land.... I wonder if the police would not forbid it, fearing that the whole country would become mentally deranged if it were used."[13]

Kierkegaard feared that we might become mentally deranged. What has happened is that we *have* become morally deranged. I believe that, to a great degree, that derangement is the result of American families becoming morally crippled by an unstructured and malnourishing diet of cable and network television. At the bottom of it all is a blind point man who either doesn't know or doesn't care that his home is under attack.

What many men don't realize is that someone or something is leading your family. Now is it you or is it television? Is it you or the peers of your children? Make no mistake, *someone* is leading. Do you know who that someone or something is?

A family needs discernment and direction. Where are they going to find it? The ideal answer is that they get it from their fathers. Without your discernment and direction, my friends, the chances are extremely high in this culture that your children will become morally deranged.

Bloom made the statement that "parents can no longer control the atmosphere of the home and have even lost the will to do so." Generally speaking, I think Bloom is right. But he was off just a hair. His statement would be much more accurate if he had said, "*Fathers* no longer control the atmosphere of the home and have even lost the will to do so."

A few years ago my son called me from the home of a friend.

"Dad, can I watch MTV?" he asked.

"No," I replied. "Son, I really appreciate your calling and asking me. I wish I could let you watch it. But there is stuff on MTV that will hurt you. I'm not going to let them do that to you. Why don't you bring your friend down here to our house, and you guys can watch one of your videos."

My son was just seven years old when he made that call. He was phoning from the home of a good family with a good dad and a good mom. I know where they worship, and it's a fine, Bible-teaching church where Jesus Christ is honored. But my question is: "Why is this guy allowing MTV to be pumped into his house to influence his three kids under the age of ten?"

It may surprise you that my seven-year-old called to ask if he could watch that program. The reason he did is because we've worked with all of our kids on this issue. If they are at a friend's house, we have emphasized the importance of calling us and checking if they can watch a particular video or program that we don't watch at home. The reason we have done this is that we have discovered some very fine people dropping the ball when it comes to television. I used to assume that I could trust the discernment of other parents. I don't make that assumption anymore. That's why I have asked my kids to call.

My son's friend has a dad who's a good guy—but doesn't control the atmosphere of his own home. Would he ever allow some sexual deviate into his home to have free reign in influencing his children? Of course not. It's amazing to me how some guys will let someone into their home to influence their kids through television who they would never allow in the front door.

Are you familiar with the MTV program *Undressed*? This is a show that *Time* magazine has described as "lust, American style." Steven Isaac of Focus on the Family offers the following on this popular program:

> *Undressed* sells sex to teen viewers. *Every* kind of sex—except that which is properly encircled by marriage. Half-hour episodes feature three separate premises: high schoolers trying to lose their virginity, college students broadening their voracious sexual appetites, and young adults shamelessly "shacking up." It's no overstatement to say that sex is the sole basis for every relationship. Undressing, touching, and caressing entwine with uninhibited discussions about sex, anatomy, orgasms, masturbation, and porn.[14]

Allow me to make a suggestion. If MTV—the network that gave us *Beavis and Butt-head*—is being piped into your home through cable, I'd like to encourage you to get rid of it as soon as possible. If you were to find that your home's water supply was contaminated with E. coli bacteria or cancer-causing PCBs, then you would take immediate and drastic steps to protect your family from the water.

If your kids have access to MTV, then they are in as much spiritual danger from the moral raw sewage as they would be from any physical danger.

Get rid of it, my friends.

Your kids may scream, yell, cry, and say that everyone else watches it. The reason their friends watch it is that they have fathers who aren't leading the family. Your first step of leadership is to cut off that vile runoff from polluted minds.

Now you may be saying, "I don't let my kids watch MTV" or "We don't have MTV at our house." That's great to hear. But may I remind you that the major networks are doing all they can do to follow MTV's lead? Think about the content of shows like *Survivor* or *Sex in the City*. The networks are only a step or two behind MTV and gaining rapidly. Personally, I don't let my kids watch MTV or prime-time network TV for the same reason that I don't encourage them to drink water from the toilet. As I write these words, groups of well-dressed executives at ABC, CBS, NBC, and Fox are sitting around walnut conference tables thinking up new ways to swim in the sewage race with MTV.

Why I am going into all of this? It's easy to look at the nation as a whole and be concerned about the overwhelming social issues. But the question is this: What am I as a father doing to keep my kids from becoming a part of these negative social issues? The only way to cut down the numbers of kids involved in everything from teen pregnancy to drive-by shootings is to get fathers involved in *leading* their homes.

Why in the world should you allow the Attilas who program the networks to come riding into your house and pick off your kids? Gentlemen, if we want to see the nation changed, then let's begin in our own living rooms.

Yes, you will probably be accused of being "strict." My kids think I'm strict. They think that because I am. When they tell me I'm strict, I immediately agree with them. And then I tell them that in twenty years when they are parents they will be stricter than I am.

This book is an attempt to help you discern the times so that you can be a better husband, a better father, and a more effective spiritual leader in your home. In an age where moral relativism, like a huge, national vacuum, has sucked away nearly every vestige of decency, truth, and goodness, it is not too late to establish those ideals in the life of your family. But it will take a godly, clear-eyed, modern-day son of Issachar riding out ahead of the family wagon.

A man who is sure and confident in the truth of the Scriptures.

A man who taps into the Spirit's willingness and ability to guide him through the moral storms that are seething just over the horizon.

America is headed for dark days, for America has crossed the line of no return. We have crossed that line morally and we have crossed it spiritually. To be quite honest, America is in deep yogurt, and there will likely be dark days ahead for those of us who hold to the moral absolutes of the Scriptures.

What your family needs in these troubled days is leadership. And it must come from you. For it is the observation of truth lived in your life that will make the difference in their lives.

But may I ask you a direct question? How about your family? How are they doing for leadership? Do they have a man at the helm who has a firm grip on the wheel? Or are things drifting?

Today is the day to stop the drift.

Today is the day to reassess your priorities.

Today is the day to begin making the Bible the center of your home instead of the television.

In other words, if you have lost control, *take* control.

Today is the day to start standing tall.

WALKING TALL

Read Proverbs 24 and discuss the following questions.

1. In verses 5 and 6, what elements do you see that could help Christian men fight the cultural war in America? How can we avoid the shame and humiliation implied in verse 10?

2. What do verses 11 and 12 have to say to Christian men who shrug their shoulders or turn blind eyes to issues such as abortion and the savage war for the hearts and minds of America's children?

3. As we wage this battle with enemies of all that is right and good and decent in this country, what note of caution does Solomon add in verses 17 and 18? Bring these two verses into today's arena, and put them in your own words.

4. What encouragement can a present-day warrior engaged in America's cultural war gain from the "big picture perspective" presented in verses 24 and 25?

5. What does the little story in verses 30 through 34 have to say to Christian men about vigilance in view of what's happening in our country? What application could we make to the "garden" of our own spiritual lives and relationship with Jesus Christ?

3

DADS WHO DRAW THE LINE

The best time to tackle a minor problem is before he grows up.
RAY FREEDMAN

The teenage son picked up the phone on the first ring.

His dad whispered, "If it's the office, tell 'em I'm not here."

That evening when the family went out for dinner, the father looked over the check and noticed the waiter had undercharged him.

"If they're not smart enough to total up a check correctly, then it's *their* problem, not mine," said the dad.

All of this didn't escape the notice of the son, whom the father had grounded just the week before for cheating on a test at school. There was nothing wrong with that boy that a moral relative couldn't take care of.

The opening chapters of this book have traced the moral deterioration of our once great nation. But it must be pointed out that every nation is comprised of individual families. A nation is only as strong as its families. That's why every family needs a moral relative at the helm. Believe it or not, history teaches that the very survival of a nation can depend upon a child having a father who is a moral relative. A dad who is a moral relative knows how to draw the lines in the necessary places.

And he also knows when *not* to draw a line.

As I write these words, Halloween is just days away. I was speaking last night to a group of men, and one of them asked me a very good question about Halloween. He mentioned that Halloween is a big problem in his family because of the origins of the holiday. In other words, because of the pagan beginnings of Halloween, he and his wife don't let their kids observe it. He then asked me what we did with Halloween.

My reply was that Halloween did have pagan origins. But in our family, when we think of Halloween, we're not thinking of anything pagan. We're just thinking about how much candy we can accumulate in about two hours. We have the mentality of chipmunks gathering acorns before the winter. We want to get as many Hershey's bars as we possibly can for the long, cold winter ahead. Our goal is to plunder the neighborhood the way the children of Israel plundered the Egyptians before they headed out for the Promised Land.

My kids have had Christian teachers who told them that Halloween was the devil's day and that they should not trick-or-treat. I did not appreciate their comments. And I did not appreciate the legalism. If you read Romans 14 and Colossians 2:16–17, you will find that some issues are issues of conscience. Some Christians observe a particular day as the Sabbath; others consider every day alike. According to 1 Corinthians 8, some Christians eat meat offered to idols; others do not (that's not a big deal in our culture, but it certainly was in theirs). Some Christians get steamed over Halloween; others plunder the neighborhood in the name of Jesus.

The point of Romans 14 is that these are issues that Scripture doesn't specifically cover. Paul says to let each man be fully convinced in his own mind. One believer will; one believer won't. Each man should have a personal conviction. But if your neighbor has a different conviction, then don't try to persuade him that yours is superior. And don't condemn him.

What I have told my kids is that Halloween does have some pagan roots. But we're not pagans. We love Jesus. To your six-year-old Halloween probably doesn't mean satanic worship. It means candy. So every Halloween I take my kids out to get candy. That's what Halloween means at my house. In other words, guys, I'm going to have to draw *enough* lines where the Scriptures *are* clear. If I don't have to draw a line, believe me, I'm not going to draw it. Especially when a Hershey's bar is at stake.

My kids aren't Satan worshipers. But they do like Hershey's bars. So we go out on Halloween and have a lot of fun getting candy; then we eat too much candy; and then we throw up later that night. We like to think of it as quality time.

PRIME TIME

Good dads have the biblical wisdom to know when to lighten up. They also know when to draw a line and how to draw a line. That's why Hollywood mocks the God-ordained institution of fatherhood.

We live in a culture where the entertainment industry consistently criticizes and belittles fathers. Michael Medved offers a commonsense analysis of Hollywood's view of the family:

> In addition to its relentless antimarriage messages that undermine the connection between husbands and wives, the popular culture also helps to poison relationships between parents and children. No notion has been more aggressively and ubiquitously promoted in films, popular music, and television than the idea that children know best—that parents are corrupt, hypocritical clowns who must learn decency and integrity from their enlightened offspring.[15]

As usual, the entertainment moguls have it dead wrong. But the Scriptures have it right. There is a script in the Old Testament that would make a blockbuster movie, but don't hold your breath for Hollywood to produce it, since Cecil B. DeMille is now deceased. Yet this is a script that every father in America should be aware of. It's the story of a man who was a moral relative. His name was Mordecai. His moral leadership in the life of his adopted little girl saved an entire nation. This is no phony docudrama or made-for-TV movie. It really happened. And it could still happen today.

The book of Esther begins with a Persian king by the name of Ahasuerus. (Some versions refer to him as Xerxes. Both names are correct.) Ahasuerus gets upset with Vashti, the queen of his nation. He gets so upset that he decides to replace her the way Richard Nixon replaced Spiro Agnew with Gerald Ford. In other words, he launches a nationwide search for a new queen. You can read all of this for yourself in the opening chapters of Esther. We pick up the story in chapter 2 verse 5:

> Now there was a Jew in Susa the capital whose name was Mordecai, the son of Jair, the son of Shimei, the son of Kish, a Benjamite, who had been taken into exile from Jerusalem with the captives who had been exiled with Jeconiah king of Judah, whom Nebuchadnezzar the king of Babylon had exiled. And he was bringing up Hadassah, that is Esther, his uncle's daughter, for she had neither father nor mother. Now the young lady was beautiful of form and face, and when her father and her mother died, Mordecai took her as his own daughter.
>
> So it came about when the command and decree of the king were heard and many young ladies were gathered to Susa the capital into the custody of Hegai, that Esther was taken to the king's palace into the custody of Hegai, who was in charge of the women. Now the young lady pleased him and found favor with him. So he quickly provided her with cosmetics and food, gave her seven choice maids from the king's palace, and transferred her and her maids to the best place in the harem. Esther did not make known her people or her kindred, for Mordecai had instructed her that she should not make them known. And every day Mordecai walked back and forth in front of the court of the harem to learn how Esther was and how she fared....
>
> So Esther was taken to King Ahasuerus to his royal palace in the tenth month which is the month Tebeth, in the seventh year of his reign. And the king loved Esther more than all the women, and she found favor and kindness with him more than all the virgins, so that he set the royal crown on her head and made her queen instead of Vashti. Then the king gave a great banquet, Esther's banquet, for all his princes and his servants; he also made a holiday for the provinces and gave gifts according to the king's bounty.

And when the virgins were gathered together the second time, then Mordecai was sitting at the king's gate. Esther had not yet made known her kindred or her people, even as Mordecai had commanded her, for Esther did what Mordecai told her as she had done when under his care. (Esther 2:5–11, 16–20)

MORAL RELATIVISM OR MORAL RELATIVE?

Every child in America needs a moral relative. A strict moral relative. And that strict moral relative should be Dad. America needs some strict fathers. There are hundreds of thousands of children walking around our schools, streets, and malls that desperately need someone in their lives who loves them enough to say no.

The first two chapters of this book outlined a rough sketch of the moral deterioration taking place in this country. May I suggest to you that one of the root causes of our breakdown as a nation is a lack of men who love their families enough to be strict.

Strict is a very unpopular word today, yet it is a very necessary word. In this nation we have lost fathers who know how to be strict—in the best sense of the term. In this nation we have fathers who are more interested in being popular with their kids than they are in being respected. And therein lies our problem.

More than forty years ago, in an effort to beat back a rising crime rate among juveniles, the Houston police department undertook a massive public relations campaign. Chuck Swindoll was a young man in Houston during this time and recounts the effort in his first book, *You and Your Child*.[16] Billboards were placed all over the city with pertinent messages to parents about raising children. One of the most well received messages was a pamphlet entitled "Twelve Rules for Raising Delinquent Children."

1. Begin with infancy to give the child everything he wants. In this way he will grow up to believe the world owes him a living.
2. When he picks up bad words, laugh at him. This will make him think he's cute.
3. Never give him any spiritual training. Wait until he is twenty-one and then let him "decide for himself."
4. Avoid the use of the word wrong. He may develop a guilt complex. This

will condition him to believe later, when he is arrested for stealing a car, that society is against him and he is being persecuted.

5. Pick up everything he leaves lying around. Do everything for him so that he will be experienced in throwing all responsibility on others.

6. Let him read any printed matter he can get his hands on. Be careful that the silverware and drinking glasses are sterilized, but let his mind feast on garbage.

7. Quarrel frequently in the presence of your children. In this way they won't be so shocked when the home is broken up later.

8. Give a child all the spending money he wants. Never encourage him to earn his own.

9. Satisfy his every craving for food, drink, and comfort. See that his every desire is gratified.

10. Take his part against neighbors, teachers, and policemen. They are all prejudiced against your child.

11. When he gets into real trouble, apologize for him by saying, "I could never do anything with him."

12. Prepare for a life of grief. You will be likely to have it.

Those twelve rules are just another way of saying to parents, "Whatever you do, don't be strict." Let me go on record as saying that strict can be very, very good. It isn't inherently bad, as many would lead us to believe in this day and age.

A family had taken shelter in the basement as a severe storm passed over their town. The radio warned that a tornado had been spotted. When the storm had passed by, the father opened the front door to look at the damage. A downed power line was whipping dangerously on the street in front of their house. Before the father realized what was happening, his five-year-old daughter ran right by him, headed for that sparkling wire in the street.

"Laurie, stop!" he yelled.

Laurie just kept going.

"Laurie, STOP!"

Laurie ran right for the enticing cable.

"STOP NOW, Laurie!"

Little Laurie reached down to pick up the wicked power line and was instantly killed.

What a heartbreaking tragedy. But the real tragedy is that it happened because a little girl had never been taught that when her father said "no," he really meant "no." It cost him the life of his daughter.

When Esther was still a little girl, she learned from Mordecai that "no" meant "no." He loved her enough to train her to obey, and that obedience not only saved her life, but the lives of all the Jews. "Esther did what Mordecai told her as she had done when under his care." Esther did not start obeying when she was twenty-one. It started much earlier than that. And it began with a man who loved her enough to be strict.

Allow me to clarify up front what strict fathers *are not*:

- Strict fathers *aren't* mean to their kids.
- Strict fathers *aren't* aloof from their kids.
- Strict fathers *aren't* distant from their kids.
- Strict fathers *aren't* physically harsh with their kids.
- Strict fathers *aren't* verbally abusive to their kids.

The kind of strict fathers that our nation needs are men who fit the following criteria:

- We need strict fathers who love their kids.
- We need strict fathers who are affectionate with their kids.
- We need strict fathers who verbally praise their kids.
- We need strict fathers who emotionally support their kids.

The strict fathers I'm referring to aren't out of balance. They are in balance. Their strictness is balanced by a host of positive qualities that give their kids an atmosphere of unconditional love and acceptance.

As a matter of fact, we are going to have to redefine the word *strict*. Dictionaries define words in different ways with slightly different nuances. I marked several variations after a brief search. Strict is:

- "marked by careful attention to relevant details";
- "incapable of changing or being changed";
- "extremely severe or stern";

- "given to or characterized by strict discipline or firm restraint";
- "conformable to a fact or a standard."

A Look at a Successful, Strict Father

Let's examine each of these definitions of *strict* one by one, for they each have something significant to offer. And let's examine them through the eyes of Mordecai.

1. Strict fathers are marked by careful attention to relevant details.

A lot of us guys are not detail oriented. But when it comes to our kids, there are certain details we need to be aware of. If you read through the book of Esther (and if you haven't done it recently, I suggest that you quickly review the book), you will find that Mordecai was always hanging around the palace gate. Why would he do that? It's simple. Mordecai wanted to know what was going on in Esther's life. He wanted to know the details. Not because he was pushy, but because he knew she was in uncharted territory. So he made himself accessible.

Some of you guys have daughters who are beginning to date. This is when you need to be aware of some details. As an example, the first detail should be "*who* is she going out with?"

Fathers in America have been removed from the dating process. It's time they got back in. *Fast*. A teenage daughter needs her father to be very much involved in this part of her life. Let me ask a question of you guys with daughters who are dating: "Do you know the guy that your daughter is going out with?" And perhaps more importantly, "Does he know you?"

My daughter began the dating process a while back. That means that I began the dating process, too. The young men who take out our daughters need to understand that we, as fathers, are going to be involved in the details. But before we get to the details, they need to understand that it is a *privilege* to take out our daughters. Not a right, but a privilege. And privileges are earned.

Does this seem old-fashioned to you? That's exactly what it is. It may not be in fashion for a father to be involved in the dating life of his daughter, but may I suggest that that's exactly why we have such incredible problems in this society? Bill Bennett pointed out that since 1962, illegitimate births have gone up 400 percent. I can't help but think that if more fathers were involved in the details of their daughters' lives, that statistic would drop dramatically.

Fathers have not been involved. They have been relegated to the sidelines. But those days are over. I can't do a lot about society as a whole, but I can definitely go against the tide of male passivity that is ruining our families and make a difference in my own family. How do I do that? By exerting some loving, strict family leadership.

I'm not talking about embarrassing our daughters, guys. I'm talking about protecting them. We obviously want to make our influence known in a way that doesn't give our daughters a reputation of having a "weird" father. And we can do that. We can get the message across without being weird or forcing the young man to sit through a cross-examination that will guarantee he never comes back.

What I am saying, gentlemen, is that your influence and presence must be realized and *felt*. There are appropriate ways to do that without putting a kid through the inquisition.

I want to meet a young man before he takes my daughter out. I want him to know that I'm interested in the details. I want to know where they are planning to go, of course, and make it clear what time I expect them to be home. And I will remind him in an appropriate way that I am trusting him to honor the plan that has been set forth for the evening and that if any pertinent changes come up, I expect them to check in with me.

If a young boy knows that a father is interested in the details, it will make a major difference in how he treats your daughter. Gentlemen, if you let him know by your actions that you consider her to be very valuable, then he will treat her accordingly—especially if he knows that you are in the picture. The fear of a father is the beginning of wisdom, especially when it comes to dating.

We should be just as involved in the details of our sons' dating lives. We should let them know that we expect them to be gentlemen at all times and to handle themselves according to a different standard than the one that many of their friends follow.

Sons should be coached by fathers—and not just in Little League. If you will take time to give your son some "tips" on how a gentleman treats a lady, then he will be miles ahead of his peers.

2. Strict fathers are not incapable of changing or being changed.

The second definition of *strict* that I found was "incapable of changing or being changed." That's a somewhat skewed definition of *strict,* in my book. Quite frankly, it needs to be changed. For the purposes of our discussion, let's alter this particular definition to "a father who is capable of changing when it is appropriate, but who has the guts to stick to his guns when he needs to." Now that definition probably wouldn't make it into Webster's, but I sort of like the way it flows. It has a nice ring to it.

Good fathers are capable of change. But strict fathers know there are times when the worst thing a father can do is alter the guidelines he has laid down. The effective, strict fathers that I know are entirely capable of change. But they know that changing the rules because a child pleads for you to do so is a very poor excuse for being an effective dad.

Mordecai was a man who taught little Esther to obey him and God. But you don't get the idea that Mordecai was overbearing. As I read this story I don't pick up any hostility between Mordecai and Esther. It seems to me that they had a very healthy relationship as adults—which tells me they had a healthy relationship while she was growing up. As the story develops, the wicked bureaucrat Haman plots to destroy the Jews. When Esther reveals the plot to Mordecai, she gives her foster dad some specific directions. The Scripture says, "So Mordecai went away and did just as Esther had commanded him" (Esther 4:17).

I get the strong sense that Mordecai was a guy who knew how to draw the line...but also had a teachable spirit. In other words, he knew when to submit. That's the mark of good leaders. They know how to submit to good counsel. I pick up the picture that Esther respected Mordecai because he was capable of change when it was appropriate.

When I was a sophomore in high school, we moved to a new town, and I began attending a new high school. It was the typical scenario of the new kid who doesn't know anyone. One of the fastest ways to make friends in a situation like that is to go out for a sport. In about two days of playing ball, you know more guys than you could meet in three months.

Normally, I would have gone out for basketball. But I had done something very foolish. I had brought home a D on my last report card. The only reason

I had gotten a D was that I had horsed around in class and basically exhibited some very irresponsible behavior where turning in papers was concerned. My dad had a rule for the three boys in our family, and the rule was this: If any of us got anything lower than a C in a class, we couldn't play ball. He didn't demand that we get straight A's or make the honor roll. My dad knew that the only reason any of us would get a D was that we were fooling around instead of acting in a responsible way.

As a result, I didn't go out for basketball. My dad was all for me playing ball. He was all-state in both basketball and football in high school, went to college on a basketball scholarship, and after World War II was offered a contract to play football for the Pittsburgh Steelers. My dad was not against sports. He wanted me to play. But he was more interested in developing my character than he was in developing my jump shot. My dad had long-term goals for me that were more important than basketball. He knew it would be good for me to have to live with the consequence of sitting out a basketball season due to my lackadaisical behavior.

One day in my physical education class we were playing basketball. I didn't know it, but the varsity coach was in the bleachers watching the pickup game. After we went into the locker room he came up to me and asked who I was and why I wasn't out for varsity basketball. I told him that we had recently moved to town and that I'd come out for basketball next year. He said that he wanted me to come out this year.

I told him that my dad had a rule about not getting any grade lower than a C.

The coach said, "But according to the school rules you're still eligible to play if you have just one D."

"Yes, sir, I realize that," I replied. "But you have to understand that my dad has his own eligibility rules."

"What's your phone number?" the coach asked. "I'm going to call your dad."

I responded, "I'll be happy to give you the phone number, but it will be a waste of your time."

This coach was a big, aggressive guy. He stood about six feet two and weighed 220 pounds, which put him one inch shorter and twenty pounds lighter than my dad. Coach was used to getting his own way. But he hadn't met my dad. I knew before the coach ever called what my dad's answer would be.

Was my dad capable of change? Sure he was. Was he going to change because he got a call from the varsity coach? Of course not. A lot of dads would have been flattered and possibly would have compromised on the consequences. But my dad wouldn't, because my dad was strict. And I thank God that he was.

That night after dinner Dad told me the coach had called. He told me that he had told the coach no. He then reminded me of the importance of being responsible in class and that he really *wanted* me to play basketball. But the ball was in my court (no pun intended). If I wanted to play ball it was up to me. At that point, I was very motivated to work hard in class so that I could play basketball the next season.

The next morning the coach came up to me in the locker room.

"I talked to your dad yesterday afternoon, and he wouldn't budge. I explained the school eligibility rules, but he wouldn't change his mind. I don't have very much respect for your father."

I couldn't believe my ears. *This coach didn't respect my father.* Even I had enough sense to know my dad was doing the right thing. Sure, I wanted to play ball, but I knew that my dad was a man of his word and that he was right in not letting me play. I couldn't believe this coach would say such a thing.

"Coach," I said, "I can tell you that I highly respect my dad. And I also want you to know that I will *never* play basketball for you."

I never did. I got my grades up, but I never went out for varsity basketball. I refused to play for a man who didn't respect my dad for doing what was right. That was the end of my high school basketball career, because that man coached basketball for my remaining years in high school.

Why wouldn't I play for him? Because he didn't respect my father. If he didn't have the sense to respect my dad, then I sure as heck wasn't going to play for him. Come to think of it, the real reason I wouldn't join his team was that I didn't respect *him.* He was a compromiser, and I suspected that he would do anything to win. My dad was a man of conviction and a man of character. And any coach who couldn't see that was not the kind of man I wanted to associate with.

My dad was strict and unwilling to change his conviction even though it hurt him for me not to play ball. My dad was capable of change, but he was unwilling to change because he had a long-term objective for my life that the coach didn't have.

The coach wanted to win games.

My dad wanted to build a son.

The issue was character.

My dad had it, and he was trying to build it into me. As far as I was concerned, the coach didn't have it. I decided to stick with the strict guy. It was one of the better decisions I have ever made.

3. Strict fathers should not be extremely severe or stern.

One definition of strict is "extremely severe or stern." Let's get one thing clear: Extremely severe or stern is not what makes for a good family. Extremely severe fathers ruin their children's lives. Ephesians 6:4 couldn't be any plainer: "Fathers, do not provoke your children to anger." Colossians 3:21 says the same thing with a different twist: "Fathers, do not exasperate your children, that they may not lose heart."

Fathers who practice the wrong kind of "strict" cause their children to lose heart. One wise scribe commented on Colossians 3:21 by saying, "A child frequently irritated by over severity or injustice, to which, nevertheless, it must submit, acquires a spirit of sullen resignation, leading to despair."[17]

There is a time to be strict, but there is also a time to lighten up and chill out. Good dads have happy homes with happy kids. Overbearing fathers tend to lose their kids as they grow older. That's a tragedy. The relationship with a child should only get better as the child develops. But that won't happen if a father is overly severe or stern.

Mordecai and Esther were close. That should tell us that Mordecai was not some legalistic nut who set stringent and unnecessary rules in Esther's life. Good dads draw the lines where they have to be drawn, but leave plenty of room for fun and good times.

Homes are like restaurants in that every restaurant has a certain atmosphere. So do homes. Most guys I know are only concerned about the quality of food when they consider a restaurant. But sometimes our wives like to go on special occasions to restaurants that have fine food and good atmosphere. Some restaurants work very hard to develop ambiance. (*Ambiance* is a classy, upscale French word—I think it means expensive.)

Have you noticed that the nicer the atmosphere in a restaurant, the greater the check at the end of the meal? Atmosphere is expensive. By the way, do you know why there are no restaurants on the moon? There's no atmosphere.

Every home has an atmosphere. And generally speaking, the atmosphere is one of two kinds. The atmosphere in your home is either *constructive* or it is *destructive*. In other words, in your home people are either built up or they are torn down. Construction or destruction. Building up or tearing down. Which is behind your front door?

Gentlemen, we set the mood. We determine whether the atmosphere is positive or negative. We can talk all day long about the deterioration of this nation, but what about your home? Are your kids falling apart under the constant stream of criticism that comes from your mouth? Are your kids having a tough time responding to you because you act one way at church and another way at home?

Let me put my cards on the table. Fathers who are overly strict are lousy fathers. Men who are rigid, authoritarian, suppressive, tyrannical, domineering, and legalistic are men who turn their kids away from Jesus Christ. Kids don't want to be around people like that. I sure don't want to be around people like that. Men who establish an atmosphere that is repressive, legalistic, and harsh are destroying their own children.

A story is told of an Persian ruler who wanted to impress a visiting dignitary. He showed the official a glass cage, inside of which a lion rested comfortably next to a little lamb.

The guest couldn't believe his eyes. "How can a lion and lamb coexist?" he asked.

"I believe that it is possible for natural enemies to find peace," replied the ruler.

"But how can a lion and a lamb possibly get along in the same cage?" asked the guest.

"It's simple," said the ruler. "Every morning I put in a new lamb."

Children are not replaced on a regular basis. That's why they must be nurtured in an environment that is firm, yet appropriately flexible. It was Sam Goldwyn, the Hollywood mogul at MGM, who said to his staff after six straight box office flops, "I want you to tell me exactly what's wrong with me and MGM, even if it means losing your job."

That's not exactly the kind of atmosphere that builds healthy relationships within a company. And it doesn't seem to work well with kids, either. Kids need strict fathers who know how to lighten up and have a good time. They don't need dads who are wound so tightly that everyone is wondering when they are going to snap. That doesn't make for a home of construction. In a nation that is falling apart, we need families that aren't.

4. Strict fathers are characterized by discipline and firm restraint.

I admit that I am reading between the lines when it comes to Mordecai and Esther. The Scripture doesn't give us a lot of details from the early years. But I am convinced that the reason Esther obeyed Mordecai later in life was that she learned to obey him early in life.

The story is told of a judge in the Wild West who had a practice of giving condemned criminals a choice between hanging and the "big, black door."

The time for execution would inevitably arrive, and the judge would go to the cell of the prisoner. "Well, what'll it be? The rope or the big, black door?" Nearly everyone who was given that option wound up taking the rope.

A sheriff once asked the judge why the prisoners always chose hanging over the big, black door. The judge replied, "They prefer the known to the unknown. People fear what they don't know."

"What lies beyond the big door?" asked the sheriff.

"Freedom," replied the judge. "But very few men are brave enough to choose the option of the unknown."[18]

A good father knows that discipline and firm restraint are the doors to lifelong freedom for his children. It is the father who chooses not to discipline that is condemning his children to lives of difficulty and hardship.

In the history of Israel is another account of a particular man who chose not to discipline his sons. His name was Eli, and his is a tragic story. Eli was a priest, yet his sons were men whose hearts were far from the Lord. Eli was one of those guys who wasn't a strict father. And it just about did him in.

The story is outlined for us in 1 Samuel 2, beginning with verses 12–13: "Now the sons of Eli were worthless men; they did not know the LORD and the custom of the priests with the people."

The account goes on to explain that Eli's sons appropriated the people's animal sacrifices for their own meals. If anyone resisted, they threatened them with force. Scripture describes their activity in this way: "Thus the sin of the young men was very great before the LORD, for the men despised the offering of the LORD" (1 Samuel 2:17).

The rebellion of Eli's sons became the talk of the town.

> Now Eli was very old; and he heard all that his sons were doing to all Israel, and how they lay with the women who served at the doorway of the tent of meeting. And he said to them, "Why do you do such things, the evil things that I hear from all these people? No, my sons; for the report is not good which I hear the LORD's people circulating." (1 Samuel 2:22–24)

Eli presented his sons with a very profound question. He asked his sons why they were doing such evil things. That was a great question. Unfortunately, Eli was a major part of the answer. Why were his sons doing such things? Listen to the words the Lord spoke to young Samuel in 1 Samuel 3:11–13:

> And the LORD said to Samuel, "Behold, I am about to do a thing in Israel at which both ears of everyone who hears it will tingle. In that day I will carry out against Eli that I have spoken concerning his house, from beginning to end. For I have told him that I am about to judge his house forever for the iniquity which he knew, because his sons brought a curse on themselves and he did not rebuke them."

Why were the sons of Eli involved in such wicked activity? Because they had a father who didn't rebuke them. Esther obeyed Mordecai later in life because she obeyed him earlier in life. Eli's sons didn't obey him because they had apparently never been rebuked by their father. He didn't rebuke them as men because he hadn't rebuked them as children. In other words, discipline and firm restraint were new concepts to them—especially when it came to their father. Boys who are not used to discipline and restraint grow up to be men with severe problems. If you have any doubt about that, just ask a prison chaplain. Why is it that our prisons are bulging at the seams? A lack of strict fathers who don't love their sons enough to exercise discipline and firm restraint.

There is an old story that has made the rounds. Two fathers of teenagers were having a cup of coffee. "Do you strike your sons?" one father asked. "Only in self-defense," came the response. There's another dad who didn't rebuke his sons early.

Skillful fathers are men who know that their children need discipline and firm restraint. Michael Green wrote:

> Loose wires give out no musical notes, but when their ends are fastened, the piano, the harp, or the violin is born. Free steam drives no machine, but harnessed and confined with piston and turbine, it makes possible the great world of machinery. An unhampered river drives no dynamos, but dam it up and you can generate sufficient power to light a great city.[19]

Strings that are tightened, steam that is captured, rivers that are harnessed, and children that are disciplined can produce astonishing results. Roy Lessin put it best: "Rules for children are like a pole that is placed alongside a tall plant growing in the garden. The pole is not there to stop the plant's development, but to help guide it into maturity and productivity."

Eli never put those poles in place, and it cost him the joy of watching his sons become mature and productive men. What a tragic waste of potential.

5. Strict fathers conform to a fact or a standard.

There is a better way of saying this. Instead of saying that strict fathers conform to a fact or a standard, it's much better to say that every child needs a dad who is a moral relative. He models the standard by his life and his behavior. He isn't perfect, but he is consistent. A father who is a moral relative is raising his children in a culture that practices moral relativism. They must see the difference in his life. That's why consistency is so important.

Ken Canfield has done some great work with fathers. One of the principles Ken emphasizes is the area of consistency:

How does a man become a more consistent person and thus a more effective father? One way is for him to understand all the different ways in which his children need him to demonstrate consistency. The research shows that an effective father is consistent in his:

- mood swings;
- presence in the family;
- keeping of promises;
- morality and ethics;
- daily schedule;
- hobbies and schedules.[20]

I see signs of consistency throughout the life of Mordecai. He might have had a temper, and he might have been impatient. I really don't know what his faults were. But I can tell you this. There was a little girl who saw enough *consistent* love in his life that she was willing to follow his counsel and put her life on the line.

Stuart Briscoe tells the following true story of leadership:

One of my young colleagues was officiating at the funeral of a war veteran. The dead man's military friends wished to have a part in the service at the funeral home, so they requested the pastor lead them down to the casket, stand with them for a solemn moment of remembrance, and then lead them out the side door. This he proceeded to do, but unfortunately the effect was somewhat marred when he picked the wrong door. The result was that they marched with military precision into a broom closet, in full view of the mourners, and had to beat a hasty retreat covered with confusion.

    This true story illustrates a cardinal rule or two. First, if you're going to lead, make sure you know where you are going. Second, if you are going to follow, make sure that you are following someone who knows what he is doing![21]

Leaders not only need to know where they are going, they need to see the big picture. It is the father's job to see the larger picture that a child doesn't see.

I recently heard a story about Earl Weaver, the former manager of the Baltimore Orioles, and how he handled his star player, Reggie Jackson. Weaver had a rule that no one could steal a base unless given the steal sign. This upset Jackson because he felt *he* knew the pitchers and catchers well enough to judge who he could and could not steal off of.

So one game he decided to steal without a sign.

Jackson got a good jump off the pitcher and easily beat the throw to second. As he shook the dirt off his uniform, Jackson smiled with delight, feeling he had vindicated his judgment to his "strict" manager.

Later, Weaver took Jackson aside and explained why he hadn't given the steal sign. First, the batter was Lee May, his best power hitter other than Jackson. When Jackson stole second, first base was left open, so the other team walked May intentionally, taking the bat out of his hands.

Second, the following batter hadn't been strong against that pitcher, so Weaver felt he had to send up a pinch hitter to try to drive in the men on base. That left Weaver without bench strength later in the game when he needed it.

The problem was that Jackson saw only his relationship to the pitcher and catcher. Weaver was watching the whole game. A case could be made that Weaver was a "strict" manager. Perhaps that's why he was such an effective manager. Weaver saw the big picture and so did Mordecai. Mordecai was a man who knew where he was going and what he was doing.

A lovely lady named Esther learned this firsthand. In the face of overwhelming odds, one man squared his shoulders and stood tall. One little girl was fortunate enough to grow up in the security of his long shadow.

The bottom line is this: His leadership ultimately saved her life. But it not only saved her life, it also saved *his* life. In fact, it saved a nation.

Every child needs a moral relative, a dad who can draw the line. And guess what, guys? We've been nominated.

Do you accept? Or do you decline? Grab a Hershey's bar and think it over.

WALKING TALL

1. What can you discern about the "father-daughter" relationship between Mordecai and Esther from Esther 2:10–11, 20 and 4:1–17? How had Mordecai's training of Esther prepared her for life circumstances that were perplexing, heartbreaking, and dangerous?

2. Review Ephesians 6:1–4, restating in your own words both sides of the parent-father "contract." What is the likely result of a dad who insists on verses 1 and 2 without providing the *context* of verse 4? What additional insight does Paul provide in Colossians 3:21?

3. Look again at 1 Samuel 2:12–17 and 3:10–14. Where does the Lord lay the blame for the evil that shadowed the sacred Tent of Meeting? What can we learn about the violence and corruption in our own culture from this account?

4. As you weigh the necessity of becoming a dad who "draws the line," carefully consider Paul's words in Ephesians 4:29–32. How do these biblical instructions modify your view of what a "strict father" looks like?

4

WHEN AMERICA LYNCHED COMMON SENSE

The Christian world is in a deep sleep.
Nothing but a loud voice can waken them out of it.
GEORGE WHITEFIELD, 1739

They were called line riders.

In many ways, it was the loneliest job on a large ranch.

The designated cowboy would load up his bedroll, fill his saddlebags, and head out to the farthest boundaries of the spread. He would then make a long circuit around the borders of the ranch. Depending on the size of the boss's range, the job could take days—or weeks—in the saddle.

Along the way, the rider made certain that cattle with the ranch brand didn't stray too far from home range and that stock from neighboring ranches didn't wander in to sample the grass. He checked the herd for sickness, noted the condition of watering holes, and kept his lariat handy in case he had to rope an adventurous cow out of a bog. Armed with a .45 pistol on his hip and a

Winchester in his saddle boot, the lonely rider kept his eyes open for rustlers, cougars, or wolves who might prey on the stock—especially the young.

Even in the years before fences began crisscrossing the wide rangelands, there really wasn't much problem with boundaries. Everyone pretty much knew where they were. The landmarks were clear: a creek, a long ridge, a butte, a stand of timber, a well-rutted trail, a wind-twisted cottonwood. There were a thousand ways to recognize the borders of the home range.

In later years, of course, the line riders became fence riders, inspecting the fences and making repairs wherever there was a break. If cattle had drifted through a break, the cowboy would round them up, if possible, and drive them back toward home.

Everyone used to know the *moral* boundaries in America, too.

We had a community that would "ride the fences," keeping watch over the young and dispatching the wolves and rustlers who had slipped onto the home range. In recent years, however, most of America's moral fences have been systematically removed.

There are even those who would deny they were ever there at all.

THE TRUE FOUNDATION

When John Hubbard, the former president of the University of Southern California, made a trip to the Middle East, he was astonished to meet so many graduates of USC halfway around the world from L.A. In the government departments alone he could count four cabinet ministers and fourteen deputy ministers as USC alumni, plus some of USC's most prosperous businessmen.

Dr. Hubbard was the guest of honor at a large banquet featuring lamb and pilaf. He brought with him the filmed highlights of recent USC seasons. One was a USC-Notre Dame game, when USC trailed twenty-four to six at the half. The robed and bearded audience groaned. The USC Trojans came back with forty-nine points in the second half to win. The audience cheered, play by play, touchdown by touchdown. When the lights went on, the host of the alumni meeting, filled with the spirit of victory, made a pronouncement.

"Gentlemen," he said, "Allah is a Trojan."[22]

That was a pretty funny line. With a room full of USC alumni in Saudi Arabia, a person who didn't know the background of USC could very easily have gotten the impression that USC was a Moslem school. The fact is that USC was originally chartered as a *Methodist* university. But most people don't know that. Especially in the middle of an alumni meeting in the Middle East.

Just as there are graduates of USC who probably don't know the historical context of the founding of USC, so are there many people today who don't realize the historical context of the founding of the United States. Allah is not a Trojan, and God is not an American. That does not mean, however, that the Word of God did not play a key role in the founding of our nation. The Bible did play a central role in the minds and hearts of the vast majority of our founding fathers.

Does that mean that America was a Christian nation? John Eldredge of Focus on the Family answers:

> If by the phrase "Christian nation" one means that every citizen of the United States at its founding was a disciple of Jesus, or required to be one, the answer is obviously "no."… If by the phrase "Christian nation" one implies that somehow the United States exhibited all of the virtues of the Christian ethic in its laws and institutions, the answer is also "no." Slavery should remove any doubt that the new nation failed to fulfill Christ's vision for humanity.[23]

We must be very careful in saying that America was a Christian nation. That is not only a loaded statement, but it is also somewhat imprecise. Eldredge hits the nail on the head when he writes that "precision is absolutely essential when discussing the role of the Christian faith in America's founding and the First Amendment in particular."

However, there is absolutely no doubt that America's founders unashamedly were shaped by the Bible in their thinking. No, this was not a Christian nation in the sense that everyone had a personal relationship with Jesus Christ. On the other hand, there was no other teaching or people who played a more vital role in the development of this nation than those who recognized the God of Abraham, Isaac, and Jacob. Quite frankly, most Americans have no idea how central the Bible was to our founding fathers.

If you have any doubt about that, you probably haven't visited Washington, D.C. Everywhere you look in Washington you see Scripture. In

Congress, you will see massive paintings that portray the centrality of Scripture. You will see Pilgrims kneeling on the soil of their new country with the Bible opened before them. You will see Scripture chiseled in marble on building after building, monument after monument. And thank God it was chiseled! Because if it wasn't, it would have been removed long ago.

When we go back and read the statements of the founding fathers, it is clear that Scripture was central in their thinking as they constructed the framework of this nation. The central book in their minds was not the Koran or the writings of Confucius or Buddha. It was the Bible. That is historical fact.

Let's ride on in and take a closer look.

A CLOSER LOOK

Just what exactly was the moral foundation of this country? As David Noebel has pointed out, "There can be no denying that the United States was originally founded on Christian principles and values."[24] In order to prove the validity of that statement, allow me to machine-gun some historical quotes and information that you probably never heard in school.

John Adams, a member of the committee appointed to draft the Declaration and a former president of the United States, says, "Our Constitution was made only for a moral and religious people. It is wholly inadequate for the government of any other."[25]

It was James Madison who declared, "We have staked the whole future of American civilization not upon the power of government—far from it, but we have staked the future of all of our political institutions upon the capacity of mankind for self government, upon the capacity of each and all of us to govern ourselves, to control ourselves, to sustain ourselves according to the Ten Commandments of God."[26]

Madison was one of the chief architects of the Constitution, yet the Supreme Court of our day would not allow Madison to post the Ten Commandments in a public school. Even though the founding fathers had staked the entire American future upon them.

George Washington made it clear where he stood when he declared, "It is impossible to rightly govern without the Bible." The beliefs of Washington are clearly documented. Much of what our kids hear today in school about

Washington is sheer myth. David Barton has written a booklet entitled *The Bulletproof George Washington*. It tells a story that was widely published and printed in all textbooks—until 1934. Because of its strong allusions to Christianity, it has been eradicated from the texts in favor of the cherry tree story.

Barton's booklet is worth obtaining to read to your family. Briefly, he recounts a fierce battle that Washington, then a twenty-three-year-old colonel, took part in during the French and Indian War. This particular battle was so intense that his life literally hung in the balance for two hours. Washington's assignment was to communicate orders from the general to the other officers in the field. This necessitated that Washington be on horseback during the entire battle. The Indian sharpshooters had been given specific directions to shoot the officers. As a result, sixty-three of the eighty-six officers were casualties.

After the battle, Washington wrote a letter to his brother, describing his acknowledgment of the hand of God that secured his safety:

> By the all-powerful dispensations of Providence, I have been protected beyond all human probability or expectation; for I had four bullets through my coat, and two horses shot under me, yet [I] escaped unhurt, although death was leveling my companions on every side of me![27]

Fifteen years later, the Indian chief who was in charge during the battle, met Washington and related to him the following account:

> I called to my young men and said, "Mark yon tall and daring warrior [Washington]?... Himself alone is exposed. Quick, let your aim be certain, and he dies." Our rifles were leveled, rifles which, but for you, knew not how to miss—'twas all in vain, a power mightier far than we shielded you. Seeing you were under the special guardianship of the Great Spirit, we immediately ceased fire at you.... I come to pay homage to the man who is the particular favorite of Heaven, and who can never die in battle.[28]

God sovereignly kept His hand on the young man who was to become a key player in the formulation of a new nation—a nation that had a unique place in the plan of God. But whatever we do, let's not let our schoolchildren hear that story! It might cause them to think that there really is a God who oversees and controls the affairs of men.

Are you familiar with John Jay? No, he didn't play third base for the Reds in 1947. John Jay was the first chief justice of the Supreme Court. He was appointed chief justice of the first Supreme Court by George Washington. Jay had this to say about the Christian foundation of the new nation: "Providence has given to our people the choice of their rulers, and it is a duty as well as a privilege and interest of our Christian nation to select and prefer Christians to be their rulers."[29]

Note that the first chief justice of the United States had no problem back then with referring to America as a "Christian nation." The influence of Christianity and the Bible had permeated every strata of life in early America, including politics.

James Wilson holds a unique place in American history in that he was one of only six men to sign both the Declaration of Independence and the Constitution. Wilson, a highly respected judge who was also appointed by George Washington, was the second most frequent speaker at the Constitutional Convention. It was Judge Wilson who said, "Christianity is a part of the common law of America."[30]

On July 4, 1776, Benjamin Franklin, John Adams, and Thomas Jefferson were appointed as a committee to prepare a seal of the United States of America. Some of the ideas they came up with show the centrality of the Bible in their thinking. Your kids, however, will never read this in their public school textbooks.

Various suggestions were offered for the design of the seal. Franklin wanted a design featuring Moses. Moses! In the background, the troops of Pharaoh would be seen drowning in the Red Sea and the message would be: "Rebellion to tyrants is obedience to God." Can you believe that? The ACLU (if it had been around back then) would have filed a suit so fast that Ben wouldn't have believed it. Jefferson suggested that the seal show that the children of Israel in the wilderness were "led by a cloud by day and a pillar of fire by night."[31]

What kind of coffee were these guys drinking? What about the separation of church and state? These were gentlemen who didn't believe in the separation of *sense* and state.

Some would object to these references by saying that some of these men such as Franklin and Jefferson weren't Christians at all. They were deists, men who believed that "God created the world as a watchmaker makes a watch, and then wound it up and let it run. Since God was a perfect watchmaker, there was no need of his interfering with the world later."[32]

Francis Schaeffer, the late twentieth-century prophet, explains the meaning of the word *Christian*.

> Not all the individual men who laid down the foundation for the United States Constitution were Christians; some, in fact, were deists. But we should realize that the word "Christian" can legitimately be used in two ways. The primary meaning is: an individual who has come to know God through the work of Christ. The second meaning must be kept distinct but also has validity. It is possible for an individual to live within the circle of that which a Christian consensus brings forth, even though he himself is not a Christian in the first sense.... Some of the men who laid the foundation of the United States Constitution were not Christians in the first sense, and yet they built upon the Reformation...to whatever degree a society allows the teaching of the Bible to bring forth its natural conclusions, it is able to have form and freedom in society and government.[33]

Most Americans are familiar with Patrick Henry and his famous statement, "Give me liberty or give me death." But there is another comment from the lips of Patrick Henry that gives particular insight into his view of the founding of America:

> It cannot be emphasized too strongly or too often that this great nation was founded, not by religionists, but by Christians; not on religions, but on the Gospel of Jesus Christ. For this very reason people have been afforded asylum, prosperity, and freedom to worship here.[34]

America was built on the foundations of biblical Christianity. Can you imagine the public outcry if Patrick Henry, John Adams, Benjamin Franklin, and Thomas Jefferson were alive today and made some of those comments in public?

First of all, they would be barbecued by the media. They would be scolded for their lack of sensitivity and accused of being messengers of hate and prejudice, completely lacking in tolerance. Newspaper editorials would label them out of touch with multiculturalism and mainstream American thought.

I can imagine that the next step would be to appoint a special prosecutor to investigate, intimidate, and instigate possible criminal proceedings for their questionable roles in such procedures that blur the line that separates church and state.

It's amazing how much can change in two hundred years.

MORAL ABSOLUTES? ABSOLUTELY!

There is no question that the Bible was the foundational and pivotal book in this country for decade upon decade. Every home had a Bible. The Bible represented the value system of most Americans. Even if someone didn't have a personal relationship with Jesus Christ, he still had a Bible and would try to live his life according to the Ten Commandments. At work and in his personal relationships, he would practice the Golden Rule.

In other words, the vast majority of Americans were directly influenced by the Bible and took their moral code from it. The moral boundaries were clear and obvious. As a result, most Americans believed that certain things were right and that certain things were wrong. They believed in moral absolutes. They believed it was wrong to lie, to steal, to kill, and to commit adultery.

In other words, they had common sense.

Have you ever referred to a friend or neighbor and made the observation that they had a lot of common sense? Sure you have. When we use the term *common sense,* what we are saying is that the person has a kind of wisdom. Common sense is a synonym for wisdom. It's just another way of saying that the person uses wisdom in making his or her choices.

It used to be that most people in America had common sense. America was characterized by common sense. You could find common sense in our schools, in our courts, and in our personal relationships. Why was that true?

Quite simply, America had common sense because we shared a common morality and a set of common values. Now the question is this: Where did that morality and those values come from?

The answer is the Bible.

The Scriptures permeated American culture. Do you see why there was such common sense in America? The Scriptures were central. But those days are over, gentlemen. It's a whole new ball game. And the rules have changed.

I recently came across a pithy little poem that summarizes the moral slide we have all witnessed. Arthur Guiterman penned these words:

First dentistry was painless,
 Then bicycles were chainless,
 And carriages were horseless,
 And many laws enforceless.
Next, cookery was fireless,
 Telegraphy was wireless,
 Cigars were nicotineless
 And coffee, caffeinless.
Soon oranges were seedless,
 The putting green was weedless,
 The college boy hatless,
 The proper diet, fatless.
Now motor roads are dustless,
 The latest steel is rustless,
 Our tennis courts are sodless,
 Our new religions, godless.

You might be interested to know that Guiterman wrote those words in 1936.

THE ASSASSINATION OF COMMON SENSE

For the last fifty years, and especially since the 1960s, moral relativism has been taught in our universities. That's why there are so many teachers, judges, congresspeople, and white-collar professionals who subscribe to it. That's exactly why America has lost its common sense.

America has had its share of assassinations. But there is an assassination that takes place every day in this country that goes unreported in the media. It is the assassination of common sense. Nearly every time I pick up a newspaper, I read of a situation where common sense has been assassinated. In fact, I have a file that is tabbed "The Assassination of Common Sense." It is to my left as I write these words. The file is packed. Allow me to pull out just a few examples.

- What should be the penalty for carrying a gun into a high school? Most of us would agree that's a very serious offense. Back when I was in high school, if a kid were to bring a gun to school, he would have been expelled on the spot. But at this writing, if a student brings a gun to school in New York City, the student will be suspended and transferred to another school.[35] Now there's a real stroke of genius. Why wouldn't they expel a kid? Because it might violate his rights. Does anyone ever think of the rights of the other kids to go to school without fear of being shot? The answer is no. That would make too much sense. Let's transfer him to another school and let him shoot a kid from another part of town.
- A man in Massachusetts stole a car from a parking lot and then died in a traffic accident while making his getaway. His estate sued the parking lot for letting him steal the car.[36]
- A burglar was robbing a school. As he was traversing the roof in darkness, he fell through a skylight. His attorneys charged the school with negligence and won $260,000 in damages plus a $1,200 monthly payment to the burglar for his injuries.[37]
- In York, Pennsylvania, after ax murderer Karl Chambers had been found guilty of robbing, beating, and killing a seventy-year-old woman, his sentence was voided and a new hearing ordered because the district attorney *quoted from the Bible*. To be more specific, in his closing remarks the district attorney said, "The Bible says, 'The murderer shall

be put to death.'" For that reason the judge ordered that the ax murderer be resentenced. I wonder how the seventy-year-old woman whom he murdered would have felt about that?[38]

- Recently in Dallas, a woman was delivering newspapers on a quiet, residential street early in the morning. She had a regular day job, but had taken on the paper route to help pay for expenses that her elderly mother had incurred. A man, recently released from a mental hospital, stepped out of the darkness, walked up behind her, and shot her dead in cold blood. Approximately one year later, as the judge released the man to freedom, he said, "Sir, I want you to do what is right. That means that you are to take your medication every day." With that, he set the man free. He walks the streets of Dallas today. Since my family lives in Dallas, I certainly hope that guy is taking his medication.

When I read of that judge's decision, I wanted the opportunity to say to him, "Judge, why don't *you* do what is right?" What he did was nonsensical. It was wildly unjust. What about the woman who was killed? What about her grieving husband and children? They never came into consideration. Why? Because we have numerous judges in this country who assassinate common sense every day.

Why did the judge let that man walk out of the courtroom? As I thought about it for a while, I came up with an answer. That judge had no fear of the Lord.

The Scriptures are very clear: "The fear of the LORD is the beginning of wisdom" (Proverbs 9:10). Would it be incorrect to say that the fear of the Lord is the beginning of common sense? I don't think so. But as America has taught moral relativism in its educational institutions, we have developed a solid line of judicial and political leaders who have lost touch with reality and common sense because they have no fear of God.

MEGADITTOES

This is getting pretty heavy so perhaps we ought to stop for a minute, go to the refrigerator, pull out a Snapple, and talk about Rush Limbaugh.

Rush Limbaugh.

The very name elicits one of two reactions. Generally speaking, if you like Rush, you probably believe in moral absolutes. If you don't like Rush, you probably believe in moral relativism.

As you probably know, Rush is the host of perhaps the most popular radio talk show in America. Literally millions of people—twenty million as of this writing—tune into Rush's "Excellence in Broadcasting Network" at any given moment of the day. When he launched his show, nobody outside of Sacramento knew who Rush was. Now they do.

I like Rush Limbaugh. I agree with him about 97 percent of the time. And so do a lot of other people who are tired of the twisted and biased coverage that comes from the majority of the media. Rush is right when he says, "I *am* equal time."

Recently I was a guest speaker at a Christian conference center. Over dinner, the conversation turned to Rush Limbaugh. The guy next to me asked what I thought about Rush.

"I think he's great," I replied.

The man was shocked. "He is such an egotist! How can you like someone who thinks he is so great?"

I explained to the man that Rush is not only a commentator, but also an *entertainer*. That's part of Rush's shtick. He does all of that "half my brain tied behind my back" stuff tongue-in-cheek. When Rush says he does it "with talent on loan from God," he's right.

As Rush explains it, this phrase is "often misunderstood by hypercritical and sensitive types to mean [I think] I am God. On the contrary, I believe that I am what I am because of the grace of God and that my time on earth, as is everyone's, is temporary. We are all on loan from God, you see."[39]

I'll be honest with you. I'm grateful for Rush Limbaugh. And so are many of you reading this book. First of all, if it hadn't been for Rush, you wouldn't have discovered Diet Snapple Peach Iced Tea. Second, if it weren't for guys like Rush and Cal Thomas, there would be very little common sense at all in the media. My one concern for Rush is that sometimes he is risqué and off-color when he's horsing around. Rush really doesn't need to do that. He's too classy a guy.

Have you ever wondered how Rush became so popular out of the blue? Have you ever wondered why this guy's program is rewriting the broadcasting record books? My theory is that Rush Limbaugh represents the thinking of the average American thirty years ago. Rush represents what America used to be like before moral relativism took over the media and education. To put it another way, Rush has common sense.

Rush has common sense because he espouses a Christian worldview—the view of the average American just three decades ago. Rush sees the world from a biblical perspective. If you read his book *The Way Things Ought to Be,* you will quickly understand that his perspective is indeed Christian. For instance, Rush makes fun of the foolishness of "animal rights" because, as he puts it:

> In my opinion, at the root of the assertion that animals have rights is the belief that animals and men are equal in creation, that man evolved from apes, and that creation is an allegorical myth contained in that wonderful piece of literature known as the Bible. There is no escaping the connection between humanism and animal rights activism.
>
> The Bible teaches that God created man in His own image and that He placed him on this earth in a position superior to all other creatures, and gave him dominion over animals and nature. God did not create other animals in His own image.[40]

Way to go, Rush. Teach that theology! Do you see what I mean? The reason he believes what he does about animal rights, abortion, homosexuality, femi-nazis, and other issues is that Rush views the world through the lens of the Christian perspective.

Wait a minute! Doesn't Rush say "damn" and "hell" from time to time? As a matter of fact, he does. And because he does, it keeps the liberals from labeling him a member of the Religious Right. I'm not condoning his language; I'm just saying that it baffles the media (as well as some Christians) to hear a guy who is not an apparent member of the Religious Right taking the stands that Rush does. Recently, Rush showed some cards in an interview with the *Wittenberg Door* that might be of interest to you.

Door: "Why are people so unhappy in this country? What does make a person happy? Where do we go to find what gives life meaning?"

Rush: "Jesus."

Door: "What?"

Rush: "Jesus. Jesus holds the answers to all of the everyday problems that you face. I am talking about an acceptance and belief in Jesus, heaven, and God. I guess you can deal with your problems on your own without those beliefs, but it's much, much tougher."[41]

Some people act like Rush is the messiah. He'd be the first to tell you he's not. He's just a guy who is speaking common sense. And now we know where it comes from.

The Separation of Sense and State

Speaking of a lack of common sense, let's look at the Supreme Court. The other day I was discussing a particular moral issue with a very fine Christian man. He is active in his church, which is a Bible-believing fellowship. In our discussion, he made it clear that although he felt that we as Christians were to definitely base our personal choices on the Scriptures, we should not be involved in the political process because of the separation of church and state. Quite frankly, I was somewhat stunned by his statement. What he was saying was that we Christians do have standards of morality, yes, but we should not impose those on others, because of the separation of church and state.

This guy has been conned. Who conned him?

Unless I miss my guess, it was the public school system, the courts, and the media.

The problem with that view is twofold. First of all, every law ever written has "imposed morality." There are laws all over America mandating that it is legal to drive only twenty miles per hour in school zones. Why is that the case? Because it would be immoral to allow someone to drive fifty-five miles per hour in a school zone! The chances are great that numerous children would be struck by fast-moving cars. Thus, in order to keep that from happening, morality has been imposed upon the populace. Every law legislates morality!

The question is this: Whose morality is going to be the standard? For nearly two hundred years in this country, the Scriptures were the basis of law. It was the principles of the Bible that held this country together. As we have seen, the vast majority of people in this country believed in moral absolutes, because that was the value system of the Scriptures. In other words, certain things were right and certain things were wrong.

But now we are fighting a battle with those who believe in moral relativism. They reject the moral absolutes of the Bible and seek to impose their morality on the rest of us. And supposedly we Christian men are supposed to stand around and let it happen because of the separation of church and state.

The separation of church and state has become the most basic principle defining religious liberty in this country. More has been done to take away religious freedoms under the guise of the separation of church and state than any other principle. But do you realize that the phrase "separation of church and state" does not appear in the Constitution? It is not found in the Declaration of Independence or in the Bill of Rights. As a matter of fact, it is not found in any legal document of this country. Read the entire Federalist Papers! It's not there. Not even once.

Then where in the world did it come from? It goes back to our friends in the Supreme Court. In 1947, a case called *Everson* v. *The Board of Education* came out before the Supreme Court. This was the first case in which the Court decided on principle of the separation of church and state. So if that phrase or concept doesn't come from any of our founding documents, then where in the world did the Supreme Court come up with it?

In 1802, Thomas Jefferson wrote a letter to the Danbury, Connecticut, Baptist Association. There were rumors that the Congress was considering establishing a national church in the United States, just as the Anglican church was the Church of England. Thomas Jefferson used the phrase "separation of church and state" to actually acknowledge the concept that had first been used by Roger Williams, a Rhode Island Baptist. In other words, Jefferson was picking up on the phrase first used by Williams to denote that it would not be proper to establish a national church in America.

In *Everson* v. *The Board of Education,* the Court presented a private letter and used a phrase from this correspondence as their bulwark reasoning in limiting religious freedom. In doing so, they violated every historical and legal precedent. So the concept of separation of church and state does not even have its roots in the Constitution. The Supreme Court had to do some shameful gymnastics to twist the true intent of the founders of this country. The separation of church and state is a result of the separation of sense from state.

Now the principle of the separation of church and state has become the bedrock legal principle in limiting religious freedom. Hitler was right: "If you tell any lie long enough, often enough, and loud enough, people will come to believe it."

THE SEMI-SUPREME COURT

Let me say a word or two about the Supreme Court.

It's not.

Do you remember when kids said "not"? I do. *Not* is a pretty good word. Especially when it comes to the Supreme Court. As I understand it, it is the Supreme Court *of the United States of America.* It may be the highest court in this land, but there is another Court that is far superior. One day, every justice who has ever served on the Supreme Court of the United States of America will kneel before *the* Supreme Court and give an account to the real Chief Justice, the Lion of Judah, for every one of his or her opinions.

Some justices, no doubt, will say in their defense that they did not want to inflict their morality on anyone else. That's no defense at all. They were never asked to impose their morality. They were responsible to be true to the Constitution. And they all swore on His eternal Word that they would do it. Some justices have been true, and more recently, some justices haven't.

Beginning in 1962, the Supreme Court began to hand down decisions that were the first legal jackhammers to penetrate our nearly two hundred-year-old biblical foundation. Since 1962, the Supreme Court has declared the following:

- Prayer in public schools is unconstitutional.
- The posting of the Ten Commandments is prohibited in public schools.
- Prayers of any type at graduation ceremonies are not allowed.
- Abortion, without consent of parents or husbands (as the case may be), is a woman's right to privacy under the Constitution.

I wonder what Benjamin Franklin and some of the other founding fathers would have thought if they could have looked ahead two hundred years to a Supreme Court that would emasculate this country by removing prayer from its classrooms.

What is the point of all of this? The point is this:

- America was founded on Scriptural principles.
- The majority of Americans believed in moral absolutes.
- There is now a new and powerful element that believes in moral relativism.
- In this new culture of openness and tolerance, there is room for any and every viewpoint except one—and it's ours.

Let me make a comment about the removal of prayer and Bible reading from public schools. The Supreme Court took prayer out of the schools, but it did not take it out of the home. The Supreme Court took prayer out of the classroom, but it did not take it out of the family. At least, not yet.

Gentlemen, you may be for prayer in the schools, but the question is: Do you have prayer in your home? You may be for Bible reading in the schools, but do *you* read the Bible in your home with your family? Those two exercises are not illegal. But to look at many Christian homes, you would get the impression that they are.

Nothing would please the enemy more than to get us all ticked off at the Supreme Court, forgetting in the process to exercise our religious freedom by praying and reading the Scriptures with our own families. My friends, if you have unwittingly taken prayer and Scripture out of your home, allow me to make a suggestion: Put it back in.

You may say, "My son plays on two soccer teams, and my daughter is in dance class three nights a week! We have no time to read the Bible every night." You don't have to read it every night. But you ought to consider doing it two or three nights a week. You may need to have your son play on only one soccer team, and your daughter may only be able to attend dance class two nights a week. I don't know how you will work out all the scheduling with your wife. *But sit down with her and work it out.* And by the way, if you do something like this, you will probably upset the coach and the dance teacher. But that's okay. There's only one person you need to please, and that's the Lord Jesus.

You are the spiritual leader. Leaders lead. Your kids need the Word of God and they need prayer. If you don't do it now when you have the religious freedom, what makes you think you will do it if we lose that freedom?

A family that is in the Book and on their knees will be blessed by God. That same approach brought God's blessing to this nation. Maybe the nation has forgotten, but guys, we can't afford to forget. This is how you protect your family. So let's turn off the TV, pass out the Bibles, and get our families on their knees. 'Nuff said.

THINKING THE UNTHINKABLE

I would like very much to put a positive spin on what I see going on around us. But it would be a wrong spin. I think that the imminent persecution of the church of Jesus Christ is blowing in faster than any of us can imagine. Gentlemen, the unthinkable is about to happen in the United States of America.

The storm clouds are rolling in.

A few years ago, in a poll of leaders across America (business leaders, government leaders, academics, priests, and rabbis, for instance), evangelicals came out the highest as a perceived "threat to democracy." Can you believe that?

Thirty-four percent of academics rated evangelicals as a menace to democracy, compared with only 14 percent who see any danger from racists, the Ku Klux Klan, and Nazis.[42] So when it comes to the menaces of society you have your Nazis, your skinheads, and the Ku Klux Klan, but leading the way are those dangerous Christians.

There seems to be a move to give everyone the right to say anything they want—except Christians. You can count on it, folks. The Left has an agenda, and they intend to do whatever they can do to silence the biblical voice, which they find so irritating and upsetting. We are the target, for we are the Religious Right.

Who comprises the Religious Right? Chances are, since you're reading this book, you do. You are an official member of the Religious Right if you believe in the authority of the Bible, the Trinity, the deity of Jesus Christ, the Virgin Birth, the substitutionary Atonement, and the resurrection of Christ; if you believe that abortion is murder, homosexuality is perversion, and sexual permissiveness is wrong; and if you agree with the statement made by Patrick Henry, then you are the new enemy in this country. For it is those principles that characterize the Religious Right. In other words, if you believe the things that the vast majority of the Founding Fathers of this country believed, then you are the problem.

You may believe that the unthinkable won't happen. Quite frankly, I hope with all my heart that you are right. But I say, *Think again.* Who would have thought fifteen years ago that the Soviet Union would fall apart at the seams? That was unthinkable, yet it is precisely what happened. Who would have ever imagined fifteen years ago that the Berlin Wall would come down? Then they were still shooting people who tried to cross that wall! Now the wall is gone. The unthinkable happened.

In the last few years we have seen some of the most unthinkable things we could ever imagine come to pass. I think that we are going to see one more. And it's one we don't want to think about.

It's the persecution of believers in the United States of America.

Two hundred years ago, most Americans did not speak of their "First Amendment rights." But they did often refer to the "rights of Englishmen." Two hundred years ago, Americans were proud to have the rights of Englishmen, and it was unthinkable that those rights would ever be taken from them.

What were the rights of the Englishmen, and why are they remarkably relevant to us? The rights of Englishmen were drawn from the various documents that made up England's constitution. The Petition of Right (1628) spelled out in detail many of the rights of Englishmen upon which the colonists were relying. More were added by the "bill of rights" of 1689. Colonists everywhere were familiar with the writings of William Blackstone, the famous common law expert whose commentaries on English law contained whole chapters about the rights of Englishmen.

From the time of Patrick Henry's famous House of Burgesses speech in 1765, through the spring of 1774, the claim to the "rights of Englishmen" led the day.

Then the unthinkable happened.

Certain powerful members of Parliament began insisting that the colonists were no longer Englishmen, or citizens. Word came to the colonists that the majority party considered them to be outside the British constitution and that their charters were meaningless. Some British leaders were saying that the colonists no longer had any rights.

The colonists were stunned. It took them months to believe and sort through what had actually happened. They were finally convinced that their appeals were falling upon deaf ears when, in August 1775, the king refused to see Richard Penn and receive the Olive Branch Petition from the colonists. That same day, the king declared the colonies were in rebellion and must be crushed. So much for the rights of Englishmen.[43]

Literally overnight, the rights, which the colonists thought to be inherently theirs, disappeared. The unthinkable took place.

It could happen again.

Allow me to take one of the above paragraphs and make a few alterations that demonstrate how quickly we could find ourselves in the state our forefathers found themselves over two hundred years ago:

Then the unthinkable happened.

Certain powerful members of Congress began insisting that the Religious Right were no longer Americans or citizens. Word came to the Christians that the majority party considered them to be outside the American Constitution and that their interpretation of the First Amendment was meaningless. Some American leaders were saying that the Religious Right no longer had any rights.

A chilling thought? Yes. An unthinkable thought? No. Not with the way things are going in this country. Consider this extract from the 1959 edition of the World Book Encyclopedia. In the article on the United States Constitution, the paragraph that specifically deals with the First Amendment contains this editorial comment:

> None of the rights protected in Amendment 1 can be considered as absolute. For example, Congress cannot prohibit the free exercise of religion, but it could pass legislation against any sect which practiced customs contrary to morality.[44]

This has already happened in America. Two different cases were brought against Christian institutions, and in each case the court ruled that the state's compelling interest in homosexual rights and racial equality overruled the First Amendment rights of the institutions. Those are two very chilling precedents. In other words, if the courts find a particular issue to their liking, they will not hesitate to use that issue to set aside the First Amendment. My friend, if you are counting on the First Amendment to guarantee your religious freedom, you are on thin ice indeed.

Until now, it has been socially acceptable to be a Christian. I think the days are coming quickly when it will be socially unacceptable to be a follower of Christ.

The lines have been drawn, and it's time to make a decision.

We either stand tall and follow Christ with all of our hearts or we don't.

It's that simple. Either get on the ark or get off.

The reason it's that simple is that up until recent times it has been convenient in this country to be a believer. But it is going to quickly become inconvenient.

We have never experienced anything like this in America before. This is a completely new chapter for us. But there are some remarkably similar parallels from history that can give us insight into what God may possibly do in our situation. More importantly, these parallels can give us hope in the midst of a new and changing high-pressure system.

Historically, whenever persecution has come to the people of God, two very positive changes have taken place:

- The church has been purified.
- The church has been empowered.

Judgment begins with the household of God. The virus of sexual immorality that has spread through its leadership has weakened the church. God is going to do what needs to be done to bring the church back to holiness. That's where persecution could come in. This won't be the first time that God's people have lived in hostile circumstances. But it's the first time that we have. And it's going to require a warrior mentality.

WALKING TALL INTO DANGER

Llamas are warriors, in their own way.

Llamas?

Several years ago, numerous sheep ranchers in a section of Montana were losing sheep to marauding coyotes at an alarming rate. The ranchers tried everything to protect their flocks. Electric fences, odor spray, and traps all failed. The coyotes kept coming. One rancher lost fifty lambs—nearly one a week—to the relentless predators.

Nothing worked. Until she got the llama. Llamas are strange-looking animals that have a warrior mentality. Llamas don't appear to be afraid of *anything*. When they see something out of the ordinary, they put their head up and walk straight toward it. The coyotes couldn't handle the courage of the llamas. So they finally left the sheep alone.

Gentlemen, we don't know what's coming. But may I suggest to you that when we see it, we lift our heads, level our gaze, and walk right toward it.

I am writing these words just several miles away from the nation's largest llama ranch. I saw quite a few of them this morning while driving to a men's breakfast. As I looked at those llamas, they had a certain aura about them that attracted me. I couldn't figure out what it was about them that made them so appealing.

But I just figured it out. The thing I like about llamas is that they are always standing tall. Literally. And because they are standing tall, they are willing to lift their heads and walk straight toward the unknown.

We, of all men, should be able to stand tall. And it's for one reason. We don't know the future, but we know who holds the future. That's why we can lift our heads and walk right into it.

The Lord Jesus has us covered.

Walking Tall

1. In what ways can alert Christian men be like the "line riders" of the Old West?

2. As you consider the message of this chapter, what new significance do you find in verses such as Proverbs 11:11 and 14:34? Looking back over our nation's history, in what ways has America been "exalted"? What is now our growing "disgrace"?

3. Carefully consider Proverbs 9:9–12. Take a moment to apply the truth of these words to our nation as whole.

4. As you soberly reflect on the probability of Christians facing persecution in our country, discover afresh Paul's description of the "last days" in 2 Timothy 3:1–5. In view of what all godly Christians must face in such a time (vv. 12–13), what is Paul's prescription for standing tall?

5. Take a moment to ponder the *ultimate* Supreme Court at the end of time as described in Revelation 20:11–15. Then turn back to Philippians 2:9–12 to consider the ultimate Chief Justice. In what way is the concept of "moral absolutes" rooted in a person? What, then, does acceptance or rejection of that person ultimately imply?

5

SHOWDOWN IN SAMARIA

It is bad to live under a prince who permits nothing,
but much worse to live under one who permits everything.
JOHN CALVIN

Since I'm a native Californian, I never expected to move to Little Rock, Arkansas. But that's what we did in 1986. And that's when I became familiar with...a certain couple.

I was somewhat aware of them before we moved to Little Rock, but it was after we settled into life in Arkansas that I began to pay much more attention to who they were and what they stood for.

Both husband and wife were deeply involved in politics. In fact, their marriage seemed more of a political alliance than a relationship. The husband sought power and was extremely ambitious. The wife sought power and was extremely ambitious. Both were leaders, and both were aggressive. He was a driven man and thought through his political moves very carefully. But, if possible, she was even *more* driven and ambitious than her husband and would seemingly do whatever was necessary to build her own power base.

This couple resided in a region where religion was popular. Part of the heritage. Part of the culture. So, good politicians that they were, they too were religious. They attended services consistently—and made sure everyone noticed.

As time went by, however, it became obvious to me that this couple's religious involvement was superficial. As I spent more and more time observing them, it became clear that their positions on moral and social issues were usually the *opposite* of biblical values. If this couple was "religious," then it was in name only. When it came to applying the truth of the Scriptures to their political decisions and choices, it was apparently the furthest thing from their mind.

The reason for this was that although they were religious, their moral and spiritual values did not come from the Scriptures. It became clear that they were primarily influenced by the value system of moral relativism that had so permeated their culture. The other thing that became plain was their deep resentment toward those who did hold to biblical morality. Not only did they loathe those who firmly held to biblical principles, but they also worked politically to make sure those biblical values (upon which their country had been founded) were kept out of the law of the land.

Whether the issue was homosexuality, the killing of children, or any other major pressing social issue, this couple worked overtime to make sure that biblical teaching had no influence on the political process. They willfully and consistently opposed those who sought to bring scriptural principles into the discussion.

As they gained more and more attention in a larger sphere, this couple made alliances with other influential groups who also stood against biblical values. It began to look as if there was no one to oppose them.

As a family, we were enjoying our time in Little Rock. But as I continued to watch this couple, I became increasingly aware of the fact that they viewed those who held biblical moral convictions as "troublesome." And it became clear to me that under the guise of "tolerance" lay what can only be described as a deep-seated hatred for the truth of God. At a certain point I realized that this couple would have no trouble wielding their power to actively stand against those who held to biblical morality.

At seemingly every opportunity, they would do whatever they could to neutralize true and godly religion and those who practiced it. At the same time, they would elevate those who practiced lifestyles of perversion to positions of power and influence and attempt to make them look good and acceptable.

Make no mistake about it: This couple was powerful. Ambitious. Shrewd. And they had an agenda.

I think by now you may have an idea of those to whom I am referring. It's hard to believe that anyone could miss this couple—especially if you are familiar with the Scriptures. Their story is outlined for us in the pages of the Old Testament.

Their names, of course, were Ahab and Jezebel.

It was in 1986, after we had moved to Little Rock, that I began studying certain sections of the Old Testament in more detail than I had ever done before. In my studies, I became increasingly aware of this couple who brought so much despair and hardship to their nation.

DON'T KNOW MUCH ABOUT HISTORY

There's an old song that says, "Don't know much about history, don't know much geography...." For most of us, when it comes to the Old Testament, that's true. We don't know much about the history of the Old Testament, and we don't know much about the geography of the Old Testament. But there is a particular clip of Israel's history that every man ridin' for the brand needs to know. And he needs to know it well.

America is in a moral and spiritual free fall. From a biblical perspective, we are unraveling at a breathtaking rate. Where we are as a country is not unlike where Israel was after the death of David. From then on, it was downhill. The glory of the former days was gone. Israel was no longer the country of prosperity and blessing that it was under David. The slide began when Solomon ascended to the throne. As Solomon began to deteriorate personally, the nation followed suit. Israel became like a gigantic, runaway snowball, picking up speed and critical mass with each revolution. That is exactly where we are today.

Maybe when you hear the word *history* you immediately tune out. When you think of history, you think of those boring classes you had to sit through in high school. Making history out to be boring should be a felony! History is the most exciting thing in the world. There is so much to learn from it. So if you're one of those guys who goes into sleep mode when you hear *history,* don't! This stuff is critical. As one great mind once put it, "Those who refuse to learn from history are doomed to repeat it."

Let's start with something most of us know a little about. How about the Civil War? Most of us could place the Civil War roughly around 1860. The Civil War was a time in history when our nation divided. We actually became two countries.

Did you know that the same thing happened in Israel? Israel had three kings. The first was Saul, the second was David, and the third was Solomon. That's pretty basic stuff that many of us got in Sunday school. But it's after Solomon that things start getting murky. That's where we need to fill in some blanks.

Why in the world would you keep reading to fill in the blanks of Israel? Unless I miss my guess, you're a fairly busy person. You have a lot on your plate. I doubt if one of your pressing needs in life is to know more about the history of Israel in the Old Testament. But listen, guys, there's a good reason to take a few minutes and check this out. If you are a husband and father, then you are leading your family in a culture that is about as morally and spiritually screwed up as it could possibly be. And right here in the era of the Old Testament kings, God has given a detailed road map that shows how to pick your way through the rubble of a collapsing society.

There's good news here, too! Even in the midst of a fast-track national decline, there were still individuals and families who did not cave in.

Instead of falling apart, they held together.

Instead of letting their culture color them, they colored their culture.

That's why this period of history is so important! It lets us know that God always has His men. Even in a time of absolute spiritual and moral decadence like ours. So let's learn a little bit of history. I guarantee that it will make you a better leader of your family.

HIGHLIGHT CLIPS

I'm a 49ers fan. However, I live in Dallas, Texas. There is a football team in Dallas known as the Cowboys. Most people in Dallas would rather watch the Cowboys than the San Francisco 49ers. So there are many Sunday afternoons when I'm stuck with the Cowboys game instead of the 'Niners. When this happens, I make sure that I tune into *SportsCenter* on ESPN. That way, I can at least catch the highlights of my team. I know that I won't get the whole game, but at least I get a few of the high spots.

That's how we are going to do this little history lesson that will make you a better spiritual leader. We are going to hit the highlights. Or to put it more accurately, the lowlights. As you will see, it was a pretty dismal time for the Israelites, God's covenant people.

We have Saul down, right? He was the first king. We have the second king down, too. David was a man after God's own heart. David had a son by the name of Solomon, and Solomon was appointed by God to be king number three. Now here's where it gets a little murky for most of us, so stay tuned to these ESPN highlights.

Solomon had a son by the name of Rehoboam (by the way, if your wife is pregnant and you are looking for a distinctive name, we are going to come across some real winners on this list of kings). Solomon had started his reign with a gift of wisdom. Unfortunately, his son Rehoboam had the gift of foolishness.

Rehoboam immediately kicks off his administration by imposing severe taxation. (Why does that sound familiar?) Jeroboam, an officer in the army, says no way and leads ten of the twelve tribes in revolt. Rehoboam was such a lousy leader that a large contingent of people turned to Jeroboam and decided that he ought to be king. Rehoboam was so hated by the people that ten of the twelve tribes of Israel backed Jeroboam. Suddenly they were a nation split in two.

The two tribes that stuck with Rehoboam were Benjamin and Judah. They were known as the southern kingdom, or "Judah." The other ten tribes formed a new nation called "Israel." For the next several hundred years, God's chosen people existed as two nations, operating under two different governments. Can you imagine the North and the South in the United States being divided for over two hundred years? Well, that's what happened here. And believe me, Jeroboam and Rehoboam were the first two of some of the sorriest leaders in history.

A CASE FOR TERM LIMITS

The seventh king to come along in the northern kingdom was Ahab. Ahab had to be one of the original inspirations for the concept of term limits. He was nothing less than a catastrophe for Israel. We are introduced to him in 1 Kings 16:

In the thirty-eighth year of Asa king of Judah, Ahab son of Omri
became king of Israel, and he reigned in Samaria over Israel twenty-
two years. Ahab son of Omri did more evil in the eyes of the LORD
than any of those before him. He not only considered it trivial to commit the sins of Jeroboam son of Nebat, but he also married Jezebel
daughter of Ethbaal king of the Sidonians, and began to serve Baal
and worship him. He set up an altar for Baal in the temple of Baal that
he built in Samaria. Ahab also made an Asherah pole and did more to
provoke the LORD, the God of Israel, to anger than did all the kings of
Israel before him. (vv. 29–33, NIV)

Ahab is remembered for two things. First, he is remembered as the
wickedest king in the history of the nation. Ahab was the guy who introduced
Baal worship to Israel. As we shall soon see, it doesn't get any worse than Baal
worship. Second, he topped that off by marrying a woman who was even
more godless than he was.

By himself Ahab would have been a menace. Plainly an opportunist,
he seems to have had few convictions or scruples. But he was not by
himself. Jezebel was at his side, using her prestige and influence as
insidiously and maliciously as possible. Like Solomon's foreign wives,
she continued her pagan worship, maintaining it on a lavish scale.
When the prophets of Yahweh opposed her heathen ways, she ruth-
lessly set out to destroy them.

Having bent every effort to suppress true prophetic activity, Jezebel
imported to her court hundreds of false prophets dedicated to Baal.
Such zeal in so strategic a position posed an incalculable threat to Israel's
historic faith. The corruption of Canaanite religion had long been seep-
ing in from the Israelites' Canaanite neighbors, but under Jezebel it was
pumped from the palace with the pressure of a firehose.[45]

Ahab did not lead his family. Jezebel called the shots in their relationship.
God has called men to lead their homes, and it follows logically that a couple
who were so set against God as individuals would also show their perversity in
their own marriage relationship. As in so many areas of their lives, they modeled

the opposite of what God intended. It started in their own marriage. Ahab was the front man, but everyone knew who was number one. And it wasn't Ahab.

A LACK OF MALE LEADERSHIP IN ISRAEL

Ahab's first mistake was marrying a woman from a foreign land who he was clearly forbidden to marry. Once they were married, he allowed her to do whatever she wanted. It was Jezebel's agenda to bring Baal worship to Israel and to make it the religion of choice. It was Jezebel who imported 850 missionaries of Baal and Asherah (a closely related cult) and fed them at her own table (1 Kings 18:19). That's an entitlement if I ever saw one.

But Jezebel was just getting started.

As Ahab gave her more and more rope, she eventually killed the true prophets of God (1 Kings 18:4). Do you see how out of control this woman was? She was the leader not only of her home, but also of the nation.

Ahab had basically given up. That's why after she killed the prophets, she did not hesitate to go after Elijah (1 Kings 19:1–2). This woman was on a rampage. And it all stemmed from a wimp husband who refused to set the standards for his own home.

What is fascinating is that Ahab and Jezebel had at least three sons—and all three of them were named after Yahweh! His three boys were Jehoram ("Yahweh is high"), Ahaziah ("Yahweh has taken hold"), and Athaliah ("Yahweh is strong").[46] In those days, children were not named loosely. I would put money on the table that Ahab and Jezebel had it out every time they had to settle on a name. Jezebel's own father was named Ethbaal, which meant "with Baal." It had to tick her off when Ahab stuck with three names that were based on Yahweh. But apparently those were about the last shreds of Ahab's waning influence. Ahab had the presence of mind in his early days to at least name his children after Yahweh instead of Baal. But as he gave in more and more to Jezebel, the influence of Yahweh on his home was lost to the influence of Jezebel.

Ahab was just one of many kings in the split nations of Israel and Judah who did not lead their families spiritually. Out of all forty-two kings, only five lived complete lives without denying or rebelling against God. The five were David, Jehoshaphat, Jotham, Hezekiah, and Josiah. Yet even the best of these men were woeful failures when it came to the leadership of their own families.

The sons of each of these good kings turned out to be disappointing failures, either with divided faith or as completely ungodly men. Thus the breakdown of godliness from father to son in even the best of Jewish homes led to increased idolatry and Baal worship in Israel.[47]

INHALING BAAL

Ahab ruled over Israel for twenty-two years. Twenty-two years under this guy! People thought it had been bad under his father, Omri. Omri ruled for twelve years, and I'm sure many folks thought it couldn't get any worse. They were wrong. Ahab came along, and it got much worse. You've heard of sons trying to outdo their fathers? Ahab was one of those sons. Unfortunately, he was successful. That's why the Scripture clearly says that he did more evil than any of the kings who went before him (including his dad).

After all these years, what is it that Ahab and Jezebel are remembered for? Ahab and Jezebel introduced Baal worship to Israel. That's their legacy. Baal worship was a very complex religion, but there are four distinguishing characteristics of Baal worship that have particular relevance to our culture.

You might be amazed at how current these four characteristics are to our own culture. Why do they sound like current events? Because America is bowing at the altar of Baal. Many of our leaders are taking us down the same path of spiritual and moral deterioration that brought Israel down three thousand years ago. We just haven't realized it.

Characteristic #1: *Baal worshipers were pro-choice.* We're familiar with pro-choice, right? These Baal worshipers were a little different. They were pro-choice *after* the child was born. They commonly killed newborn children in the worship of Baal.

Characteristic #2: *Baal worshipers held the environment in high esteem and considered Baal as the one who determined and controlled the environment.*

Characteristic #3: *Baal worship encouraged and promoted rampant sexual immorality, particularly homosexuality, as a normal and natural alternative lifestyle.*

Characteristic #4: *Baal worship sought to coexist as a legitimate religious viewpoint alongside Judaism.*

Let's take these one by one, for all can be found in the account that describes Israel under the leadership of Ahab and Jezebel. Let's go back to characteristic #1.

Characteristic #1: Baal Worshipers Were Pro-Choice

Immediately after introducing Ahab and Jezebel, the Scriptures then describe what seems to be a very weird situation that doesn't have much to do with Israel. But it is very significant.

> In Ahab's time, Hiel of Bethel rebuilt Jericho. He laid its foundations at the cost of his firstborn son Abiram, and he set up its gates at the cost of his youngest son Segub, in accordance with the word of the LORD spoken by Joshua the son of Nun. (1 Kings 16:34, NIV)

This passage is a reference to the man who attempted to do what God said would never be done. He attempted to rebuild Jericho but was foiled, for God said Jericho would never be rebuilt. This attempt took place during the reign of Ahab. But what should be noted is the fact that Hiel possibly buried his sons in the foundations of Jericho. It appears to have been a practice of Baal worshipers not only to kill their newborn children, but also to bury them in the foundation of a house or wall. Archaeologists have found the remains of several small children in the ancient ruins of homes and fortified walls.

Baal worshipers were also known for making their sons pass through the fire. This even became a practice in Israel after Ahab introduced Baal worship to the nation. The point is this: Human life was cheap in Israel and Judah, and it is cheap in America. Generally speaking, we don't practice the killing of infants (although some doctors have done it after a botched abortion), but we do sanction the killing of children in the womb.

As I write these words, there is controversy in our country over the practice of partial-birth abortions. These are late-term abortions in which a baby is partially delivered, then killed. Several states have passed bans on partial-birth abortions, but many of these have been struck down by the courts. What this means is that doctors can legally abort a baby just fifteen minutes away from birth. What is the difference between killing a baby fifteen minutes before birth or killing it fifteen minutes after birth? About thirty minutes. That's the only difference.

Life is cheap in America. Yet as a nation, we know in our hearts what we are doing. Those aren't fetuses; they are babies. In a revealing article in the *Dallas Morning News*, Janie Bush, director of the Choice Foundation, made the following astonishing admission:

> We have learned a great deal from the movement that calls itself pro-life. We were hiding [from ourselves and other women] some pieces of the truth about abortion that were threatening. It is a kind of killing, and most women seeking abortion understand that.

Ms. Bush's amazingly candid admission was not well received by other abortion advocates. Kate Michelman, president of the National Abortion Rights Actions League said, "I would never tell someone they are killing. It is a loaded term." So what would Ms. Michelman tell them? She would say that "they are terminating a stage of fetal development and potential life."[48]

Ms. Bush was very honest in her comments. So honest that her peers could not handle it. They are experts in denial. I wonder how Ms. Michelman would have justified the sacrifice of newborns in Ahab's day. If we keep going the way we are, in a few years we will find out.

The point is simply this. In the spiritual deterioration of Israel, the killing of children was acceptable behavior. No wonder we witness the same spirit in our nation as we continue to watch our moral infrastructure erode.

A few years ago, then–Vice President Al Gore, in his book *Earth in the Balance,* registered his concern over the burning of the rain forests. Gore wrote, "According to our guide, the biologist Tom Lovejoy, there are more different species of birds in each square mile of the Amazon than exist in all of North America—which means we are silencing thousands of songs we have never heard."[49] It is somewhat baffling that a family man such as Mr. Gore would be so concerned about the songs that would not be heard from birds and apparently so unconcerned about the songs that aborted babies will never have the opportunity to sing.

Birds are important, but they can't hold a candle to children. I like to hear the songs of both, for each has been created by God to sing. But children are superior to birds and more important than birds. At least that's what Jesus taught: "Look at the birds of the air, that they do not sow, neither do they reap, nor gather into barns, and yet your heavenly Father feeds them. Are you not worth much more than they?" (Matthew 6:26).

Jesus made it very clear that human life is more important and more valuable than the life of a bird. Unfortunately, it doesn't seem to be as clear to some leaders in today's society.

Characteristic # 2: Baal Worshipers Were Obsessed with the Environment

Baal worshipers held the environment in high esteem and considered Baal as the one who determined and controlled the environment. Elijah tackled that issue the very first time he went one-on-one with Ahab.

> Now Elijah the Tishbite, from Tishbe in Gilead, said to Ahab, "As the LORD, the God of Israel, lives, whom I serve, there will be neither dew nor rain in the next few years except at my word." (1 Kings 17:1, NIV)

There is more here than meets the eye. Elijah is not just showing up to give Ahab the latest forecast from the Weather Channel. Elijah is laying down a challenge and stating a fact. Now this was the first public appearance of Elijah. Up until now, he was just some guy from Tishbe. But never again could he fade into the scenery. Elijah was a marked man because he had taken on Ahab. But more importantly, he had taken on Baal.

Why did Elijah talk to Ahab about the weather? He could have addressed a number of issues, but why the weather? The answer is this: Ahab and the other Baal worshipers thought that Baal was the one who controlled the weather. And they worshiped him as such. But they were wrong.

Baal was known for his many strengths, but primarily he was known as the storm god: "As the god of the storm, whose voice resounded through the heavens in the form of thunder."[50] Elijah was stealing Baal's thunder. "Baal was a god of many faces, being a god of rain, fertility, and the personification of the sun."[51] To be more precise, Elijah was challenging Baal's ability to make thunder, and then rain.

Oswald Sanders wrote:

The worship of Baal...one of the oldest superstitions in the world, was the worship of the sun, regarded as the king of heaven. The Baalim were the gods of the land, owning and controlling it, and the increase of the crops, fruit, and cattle was supposed to be under his control.[52]

We're talking the environment here, guys.

Baal worship was all wrapped up in depending upon Baal to take care of the environment. Baal worship was built around the environment. They worshiped the creation over the Creator. They put a high value on animal life and the ecosystem while discounting human life the way that Wal-Mart might discount a bag of Oreos.

This stuff has been around for a long time. We are not the first culture to have a vocal group that seeks to elevate the environment to a place of deity. The animal rights activists and ecology groups of our time are the modern day equivalent of Baal worshipers. They have a value system, just as the prophets of Baal had a value system, and they are working feverishly to get their curriculum and influence into our schools, our movies, and our kids' cartoons.

In other words, they want the minds of our children.

Let me give you one more illustration from Al Gore on the environment. In arguing for the preservation of the rain forest, Gore says,

> If we allow this destruction to take place, the world will lose the richest storehouse of genetic information on the planet, and along with it possible cures for many of the diseases that afflict us. Indeed, hundreds of possible medicines now in common use are derived from plants and animals of the tropical forests. When President Reagan was struggling to survive his would-be assassin's bullet, one of the critical drugs used to stabilize was a blood pressure medication from an Amazon bush viper.[53]

So far, so good. That's a good reason not to have the wholesale destruction of the rain forest. I agree with his point. It makes sense to me that we were able to save Mr. Reagan's life because of the medicine that was derived from the bush viper. So let's save the rain forest in order to get medicines from plants and animals to save human lives. Doesn't that seem to be his point here? Well, hold on for the very next paragraph.

Most of the species unique to the rain forests are in imminent danger, partly because there is no one to speak up for them. [Farrar editorial comment: Once again Mr. Gore is very concerned about speaking up for something like a bird or a tree which can't speak. Why isn't this man consistent in giving the same concern to unborn children as he does to the yew tree?] In contrast, consider the recent controversy over the yew tree, a temperate forest species, one variety of which now grows only in the Pacific Northwest. The Pacific yew can be cut down and processed to produce a potent chemical, taxol, which offers some promise of curing certain forms of lung, breast, and ovarian cancer in patients who would otherwise die.

It seems an easy choice—sacrifice the tree for a human life—until one learns that three trees must be destroyed for each patient treated, that only specimens more than one hundred years old contain the potent chemical in their bark, and that there are very few of these yews remaining on earth. Suddenly we must confront some tough questions. Are those of us alive today, entitled to cut down all of these trees to extend the lives of a few of us, even if it means that this unique form of life will disappear forever, thus making it impossible to save human lives in the future?[54]

It is here that Mr. Gore reveals the true colors of his position. Mr. Gore speaks of the tough questions. Quite frankly, these questions are not tough at all. They are only tough if you buy into a philosophy that puts people and trees on the same playing field. Mr. Gore points out that it is an easy choice to sacrifice a tree for a human life—until one realizes several things:

- In actuality it takes three trees to save a life.
- The tree must be over one hundred years old.
- There are few yew trees left.

According to Gore, here's where it "gets tough." Allow me to offer some answers to Mr. Gore.

Question: Are those of us alive today entitled to cut down all of these trees to extend the lives of a few of us?

Answer: *Yes.* Mr. Gore speaks of the few whose lives would be extended. That's an interesting comment. The few of whom he speaks are those who suffer from lung cancer, breast cancer, and ovarian cancer. For some reason, the number of people suffering from such diseases strikes me as more than a few. My field is not medicine, but it would be my guess that thousands, if not hundreds of thousands, of people fall within the confines of those three types of cancer.

What if the yew tree was a known cure for AIDS? Would Mr. Gore have the same reservation about "sacrificing" the tree in that case? For some reason, I have my doubts. Or what if it were discovered that the yew tree was the only resource for a mysterious illness that was killing off thousands of dolphins? Would the former vice president still be facing some tough questions? I think it's possible that Mr. Gore and his friends would be oiling their chain saws as quickly as possible in an attempt to save as many "Flippers" as they could. But humans suffering with cancer? Well, that's a tough one.

I can say this. If my wife, or one of my children, was suffering from one of those forms of cancer, and the cost was three trees, then that is a no-brainer. Quite frankly, if it were three hundred trees—or a *forest*—I would not hesitate. It wouldn't be tough at all. I sincerely doubt that Mr. Gore would hesitate to bring down three hundred trees if it meant sustaining the life of one of his loved ones.

Question: Are we entitled to cut down all of the yew trees, even if it means that this "unique" form of life will disappear forever, thus making it impossible to save human lives in the future?

Answer: *Yes.* We are entitled because if you believe that the Scriptures are God's divine revelation, God makes it clear that He has given mankind dominion over the earth. Men and women, boys and girls, infants and unborn children are made in the image of God. Trees aren't.

The yew tree may be "unique," but it is not nearly as "unique" as any person who walks this earth. And how do we know that if the yew trees are saved they would be sacrificed in the future to help meet the needs of people?

Excuse me for going into such detail, but, gentlemen, we need to understand that these beliefs have very serious implications. The modern-day environmental movement is committed to cutting no trees down, regardless of whom it might harm. Therein lies the danger: They have elevated the earth to the same plane as people. That is wrong. It is simply another form of Baalism that is just as insidious and dangerous as its philosophical ancestor in Israel.

Why in the world are we talking about trees in a book that is aimed at men who want to spiritually lead their families? We are talking about it because our children are being bombarded every day with this extreme environmental garbage that is both inhuman and ungodly.

Now let me set the record straight. I'm all for trees, and I'm all for the environment. I just spent four hundred dollars in an effort to save two pecan trees in my front yard. I like those trees. They are beautiful and majestic. But they are not as important as people. Should we destroy the earth and be irresponsible with our stewardship? Of course not. Adam was told to subdue the earth, not ruin it. But should we forget that people are made in the image of God while animals and trees are not? Of course not. Yet that's exactly what we're doing. And the fingerprints of Baal are all over that kind of thinking.

Gentlemen, we need to teach our kids the truth about the environment from the Scriptures. Take them back to Genesis and show them that God created the world. Show them that God then created man and gave man authority over the creation. Show them that people are made in the image of God. In other words, guys, give your kids a biblical perspective so that they can fight off this dangerous and deceptive worship of the environment that destroys the lives of people. Teach them the Word of God, and you will give them a foundation on which they can stand tall and fight off the false teachings about pro-choice and the environment that are a direct perversion of God's plan for the earth. Read through Francis Schaeffer's classic treatment of the environment, *Pollution and the Death of Man*. It will give you a balanced presentation that you can adapt as you talk to your kids about these issues.

We have only covered two of the four characteristics of Baal worship. We'll hit the last two in the next chapter. And believe me, it gets worse. Much worse. But I think you're probably starting to get a flavor for this insidious belief system that brought down Israel. Perhaps "flavor" is a poor choice of terms. I think Elijah might refer to it as a "stench."

It was Elijah whom God used to confront Ahab and Jezebel over the issue of their wicked leadership in Israel. We will devote an entire chapter to Elijah later in this book, but suffice it to say that Elijah could spot a Baalist at fifty miles. And he could smell one from a hundred.

What do you think the reaction of Elijah would be if he were to make an appearance in the United States of America in the early twenty-first century? I think he would immediately pick up the stench that now permeates virtually every part of this nation. He could walk from sea to shining sea and see the spiritual devastation that accompanies the presence of Baal. Most Americans don't even know who Baal is, let alone what he stands for. But Elijah does. And I wouldn't be surprised if he were to make his way to the capital of this nation as he once made his way to the capital of Israel. And for some reason I have the sneaking suspicion that his message would be the same message of God's judgment.

And because Elijah was such a straight shooter, I think he would deliver his message to any and all of our leaders who have bowed to Baal. He would declare it to the executive branch, the legislative branch, and the judicial branch. He would tell it straight to Democrats, Republicans, and Independents alike. He would ignore such religious affiliations as Methodist, Baptist, Episcopalian, Roman Catholic, or any other denominational tag. You see, back when Elijah spoke for God, there were no denominations. You were either on the Lord's side or you weren't. You either submitted to the authority of God or you didn't. You either promoted the holiness of God or you mocked it.

That's why Elijah could spot a Baalist at fifty miles. The lines were clearly drawn. And I think Elijah would quickly and powerfully redraw those lines for our leaders who have erased them like a lead-off hitter who takes his foot and deliberately wipes away the chalk in a freshly marked batter's box.

I think Elijah would immediately detect that the same forces that destroyed Israel are destroying us. And that's why he would stand tall, redraw the lines, and courageously remind our leaders that the sovereign and immutable God of Abraham, Isaac, and Jacob is still calling the shots. He might even quote Psalm 2:10–12:

Now therefore, O kings, show discernment;
Take warning, O leaders of the earth.
Worship the LORD with reverence,
And rejoice with trembling.
Do homage to the Son, lest He become angry,
    and you perish in the way,
For His wrath may soon be kindled.

WALKING TALL

1. Briefly review the steep downhill slide on which Israel found itself because of its evil leadership. Check out 1 Kings 16:12–13, 18–19, 25–26, 30–33. What kind of trend do you see here? In your view, is America at the beginning of such a trend…or are we already quite a way "down the slide"? Explain your answer.

2. Elijah stood tall in the face of terrible evil and terrible danger (1 Kings 17:1–9). Why do you suppose God suddenly pulled him from the front line and gave him an extended time of R&R? As Christian men face the intensity of an emotionally exhausting, sometimes dangerous cultural warfare in our country, how can we find a balance between fighting the good fight and simply enjoying life with our families?

3. Review the Creator's intentions for man and his "environment" in Genesis 1:26–29 and 2:15, 19–20. How has today's environmental movement twisted God's mandate for the world? What can we as dads do to help our kids stand tall against the nonstop brainwashing on this issue that so saturates our culture?

4. Look back in this chapter at the first two characteristics of Baal worship. How long ago did these "warning signs" appear in our country in a major way? In what ways do you see them growing more and more prevalent as time goes by?

6

HIGH NOON
FOR A NATION

GAY WRONGS, PART 1

When principles that run against your deepest convictions
begin to win the day, then battle is your calling, and peace has become sin;
you must, at the price of dearest peace, lay your convictions bare before friend
and enemy, with all the fire of your faith.
ABRAHAM KUYPER

I
n the classic 1952 western *High Noon*, Gary Cooper gives an Academy Award–winning performance as a U.S. marshal awaiting the arrival of four vengeful gunmen bent on shooting him down.

Three of the killers clean their guns and bide their time at the station. The train bearing their leader is scheduled to roll into the placid little desert town at twelve o'clock.

High noon.

Throughout the taut drama, director Fred Zinneman skillfully and repeatedly intersperses the action with two haunting images. The first image is that of empty train tracks stretching off into a heat-distorted horizon. Down those tracks, just out of sight, a relentless evil is bearing down on a peaceful town.

The second image is that of ticking clocks. Lots of clocks. Wall clocks. Grandfather clocks. Desk clocks. Pocket watches. All of them ticking down the hours and minutes and seconds until the howling locomotive rolls into the station bearing bitterness and death for a good man who must stand alone against the evil, against the odds.

Throughout the movie, Cooper approaches citizen after citizen, appealing for deputies to stand beside him as the inevitable showdown draws nearer. No one is willing to risk his life. Not even the men he called "old friends." At the eleventh hour, Cooper interrupts the Sunday service of the town's church. These are good people, he reasons, people who ought to be willing to stand tall against the shadow creeping toward their town. The pastor, however, finds himself in a moral dilemma and can't recommend anything. The mayor rises to counsel prudence and suggests that the marshal simply flee. The men in the church debate the issue, leaning first this way, then that way—paralyzed by timidity and indecision. In the end, Cooper walks out alone.

He loves life. He would love to leave on his honeymoon with his new wife (you would too if you'd just married Grace Kelly), but he knows in his heart he can't run. He has to take a stand, even though it will most likely mean his life.

One jaded old lawman, played by Lon Chaney, tells Cooper the bitter truth: "People don't care. They just don't care."

An interesting thing happened as Warner Brothers filmed the fateful approach of the noon train. They just about lost their cameraman.

He was lying on his stomach in the middle of the tracks focusing on the locomotive rushing in from the horizon. It was such a dramatic shot. The train rushed closer and closer, billowing white smoke. Then, as it drew nearer, it billowed black smoke. What a great effect! The cameraman was relishing every exciting frame. What he didn't understand was that the black smoke was meant to be a *distress signal*. The train had lost its brakes.

Looking through the lens, he watched the death train hurtle toward his camera. But wasn't the engineer overdoing it a little on the whistle? And why wasn't he hearing the squeal of brakes? And my goodness, the thing didn't seem to be slowing down! At the last possible second, the cameraman hurled his camera to one side and leaped off the tracks as the locomotive screamed right on through the station. The camera was destroyed by the impact, but the film cartridge remained intact. Fortunately, so did the cameraman.

Gentlemen, I don't mean to sound theatrical or melodramatic, but it is high noon for America. In fact, it may be closer to twelve-thirty. An unbelievably destructive evil has rolled into our cities and towns and communities, bringing death, perversion, and the destruction of many cherished values and ideals. We'll talk about that evil in the next two chapters.

Yes, it may be too late to stop the train, but it's never too late for good men to make a determined stand in defense of their homes and families.

We need men who are willing to stand tall, and we need them now.

Why now?

In our last chapter we saw how our nation has fallen into the same kind of Baal worship that seduced and ultimately destroyed the northern kingdom of Israel. We zoomed in on the first two characteristics of Baal worship:

#1. Baal worshipers were pro-choice after the child was born.

#2. Baal worshipers held the environment in high esteem and considered Baal as the one who determined and controlled the environment.

In this chapter, we will consider the last two traits of Baal worship:

#3. Baal worship encouraged and promoted rampant sexual immorality, particularly homosexuality, as a normal and natural alternative lifestyle.

#4. Baal worship sought to coexist as a legitimate religious viewpoint alongside Judaism.

TIME CHANGES ITS TUNE

I recently came across a somewhat inflammatory statement about homosexuality. Instead of letting you know who made the statement, allow me to quote it…and then let's talk about the source:

> Even in purely nonreligious terms, homosexuality represents a misuse of the sexual faculty and, in the words of one…educator, of "human construction." It is a pathetic little second-rate substitute for reality, a pitiable flight from life. As such it deserves fairness, compassion, understanding, and, when possible, treatment. But it deserves no encouragement, no glamorization, no rationalization, no fake status as a minority martyrdom….

Now who made the statement? Let's make it multiple choice. Was it:

A. Pat Buchanan.

B. Jerry Falwell.

C. Rush Limbaugh.

D. An essay in *Time* magazine.

The answer is D. It is a direct quote from an issue of *Time* that I recently came across. I couldn't believe my eyes. I did not expect that kind of thinking from *Time*. That's when I noticed the date of the issue.

January 21, 1966.

If an editor at *Time* were to make a statement like that today it would be the end of his journalistic career. He would be ostracized from the honorable practice of free expression forever. The reason he would be ostracized is that free expression in the American press is, generally speaking, a thing of the past. That statement would never appear in *Time* because it is not politically correct. The problem with the paragraph is that it does not speak of homosexuality in glowing terms. And that is a problem! According to the writer, "homosexuality is a pathetic little second-rate substitute for reality." That is not acceptable in *Time* or in any other self-respecting news magazine of the year 2000.

In America in the twenty-first century, homosexuality is not "second-rate"; it is first-rate. And not only is it accepted, it is encouraged. And God help the writer at *Time* or any other newsmagazine who would dare to differ.

I recently spent some time on a Saturday at the library of a major university. I was sitting at a computer in the periodical section doing a literary search of articles written on homosexuality. I started in the 1950s and worked my way up to the 1990s. It was one fascinating ride through the annals of American thought. What I discovered was this: Up until 1968, the reporting in *Time* and other popular magazines concerning homosexuality reflected a value system that was based on moral absolutes. In other words, the writers at *Time* were working from a framework of Judeo-Christian moral absolutes that viewed homosexuality as wrong and abnormal.

That all changed with one article in 1968. In that one article, *Time* made an amazing leap to the viewpoint of moral relativism. With one stroke of the pen, *Time* was on a crusade to not only approve homosexuality, but to justify it.

HOMOSEXUAL RIGHTS:
COMING SOON TO A CITY NEAR YOU

This is a book to Christian men. And what Christian men need to understand is that the greatest moral threat to your family in this country is militant homosexuality.

We'll talk about that, but first allow me to make an important distinction. I have met some very fine people who have struggled with the issue of homosexuality in their lives. It is something they know is wrong and many of them have taken significant steps to bring this issue of their lives under the control of the Holy Spirit.

I know of others, who, after pursuing the gay lifestyle for a time, turned to Christ as a result of discovering they have AIDS. They regret their past behavior and have repented of it at the foot of the cross. They have met Jesus Christ as their Lord and Savior.

I had breakfast with a friend this morning. My friend's brother, who lives in another state, is dying of AIDS. But as my friend described it, his brother has received a transfusion of the blood of Christ, and he has received eternal life.

I know people who have deeply struggled with homosexual tendencies in their lives and continue to struggle. They have my most sincere concern and sympathy. As I have met with them in the confidentiality of counseling sessions, I have assured them that I am on their team. Some of you reading this have struggled firsthand with homosexuality because of a missing emotional piece in your relationship with your father. The only response to a man who is working through this issue is biblical love and compassion.

But there is another group who demands that their actions be accepted and approved. Any hesitancy to do so prompts them to cry either "bigot" or "homophobe." These are the *militant* gays. We are talking about a very powerful and wealthy group of individuals who have a clear strategy and agenda. Try as they may to cloak that agenda in the media (since it isn't socially acceptable), their goals have been clearly spelled out in print by their own writers. In a nutshell, the militant homosexual community desires to bring about two radical changes to our society:

1. They want to remove the sodomy laws from the books.
2. They want to remove the age of consent laws from the books.

For all intents and purposes, they have effectively achieved their first goal. For even in states where sodomy laws are still in effect, they are conveniently ignored by the authorities.

What is frightening is their desire to remove the age of consent laws from our legal framework. Now, I want to be fair on this point. Not all homosexuals want to lower or remove the age of consent laws. However, after reading the literature of the gay rights movement, one can only conclude that for what appears to be a significant and vocal number, that is indeed their aim.

I find that many Christian men are ignorant of this side of the homosexual agenda. Quite frankly, the ramifications of such a change are so staggering and so wicked that they defy description. But make no mistake. This is the agenda. It's high noon, gentlemen, and this is no time to be naive.

I recently had a Christian father tell me that he was more concerned about someone speeding down his residential street than he was about the homosexual agenda. This man, though highly educated, is not thinking clearly. He has completely fallen for the homosexual propaganda that flows out of the media with the steady and unrelenting pressure of a fire hose. Of course this father should be concerned about speeding cars in his neighborhood. That is an apparent threat to his children. But he should not be unaware of the hidden threat of the gay agenda.

If your reaction to what you are reading is: "This is homophobic, reactionary, alarmist, or hateful," then you, my friends, have also been taken in. And you will live to see the day that you regret it.

Let us make no mistake about it. Gay rights is not about the normative rights that all citizens enjoy. Men and women who practice homosexuality have the same rights as those of us who don't practice homosexuality. Gay rights is about *special rights*. It is these special rights that will ultimately bring down judgment upon this nation.

Why am I writing about militant homosexuality in this book to men? I am writing about it because it's an issue that you will soon have to face in your community. It's an issue that you can't escape. The train has already rolled into town. The destroyers are already in the streets.

I have met Chuck McIlhenny on several occasions. Chuck is a levelheaded man who loves his family and the church that he pastors in San Francisco. I like Chuck because he, too, rides for the brand. He is a man of courage who has stood tall for the truth against unbelievable opposition. His home and church have been firebombed; he has been sued on more than one occasion; and his children have been threatened sexually. Here's what Chuck says to those of us who don't live in San Francisco:

> Whether you want to or not, you will eventually have to deal with the gay rights movement. It may first appear as a "human rights ordinance" at your local city council; or it may turn up as a pro-homosexual teen counseling center at your local junior and senior high school, or perhaps as a safe-sex education program for your children, teaching them that homosexual sex and same-sex partnerships are just as "normal" as heterosexual marital relationships. All of these things are in effect in San Francisco at the present time. Regardless of how it comes to your community, you and your children will eventually be *forced* to submit to the homosexual agenda—or face legal sanctions.[55]

Chuck knows firsthand of what he speaks. I know of two other men who have also paid a tremendous price for taking a moral stand on the issue of homosexuality. Both men were in highly visible positions in two of America's largest cities. Although their competency and excellence in their respective positions were beyond reproach, they were both the objects of direct and concerted public campaigns to drive them from their positions. Both men were relieved of their duties because they dared to stand in opposition to the homosexual agenda.

Now what we should understand is that neither one of these men went out of their way to take on the homosexuals. They didn't picket anybody, they didn't lead a demonstration, and they didn't file a lawsuit. They were persecuted and eventually railroaded out of their positions because somewhere in the normal course of their life they stated in a way *unrelated* to their jobs that they opposed homosexuality on moral grounds.

How did homosexuals get so much power?

How did a sexual practice that even *Time* magazine considered to be less than normal thirty-five years ago gain such prominence and clout? Roger Magnuson speaks of "a great iron triangle of a special-interest group [the homosexual lobby], the media [filled with issues consultants], and compliant legislators who ensure that programs are sensitive to homosexuals."[56]

Let me reiterate what I said previously. If you think that I am panicking, resorting to hyperbole, or overstating my concerns, then you are the very man who needs to read on. How did a group that was outside the boundaries of morality just ten, fifteen, or twenty years ago suddenly become mainstream? How is it that anyone who dares to speak in opposition is looked upon as prejudiced, hateful, and intolerant? If the homosexual movement has gained this much power in the last twenty years, how much more will it gain in the next twenty?

Chuck McIlhenny issues a warning:

The homosexual movement is coming after your right to free speech, to religious freedom, and, most importantly, after your public school children through homosexual recruitment programs disguised as "safe sex" and/or AIDS education classes, alternative lifestyle classes, or through counseling services for teens run exclusively by gays and lesbians. And, no, your private Christian school will not be spared if anti-discrimination/sexual orientation ordinances are passed in your community. There will be no exceptions allowed in their bid for political rule over community after community—and why should there be? These are two mutually exclusive moralities; one based on the Word of God, and the other based on the arbitrary will of men.[57]

Once again, we are back to the clash between those who believe in moral absolutes and those who believe in moral relativism.

What will you do if your state passes a law that prohibits "discrimination" against homosexuals or any adulterer, and even includes a prohibition against speaking or writing anything critical of such immoral conduct? Will your church take a stand? Will your pastor take a stand? Will you support your pastor if he does take a stand, even though your reputation in the community may suffer? Or will you compromise and allow legislated immorality to take over your community in the name of freedom? Will you allow your children to be recruited by such ungodliness in your tax-funded public schools and organizations? Only you can answer these questions.[58]

Georgia on My Mind

Marietta, Georgia, is a peaceful, family-oriented suburb just north of Atlanta. A recent *USA Today* article describes what happened when two thousand gay activists swarmed the town square park to protest the passage of legislation in Cobb County declaring homosexuality "incompatible with community standards." The homosexuals took over the park, which is usually a haven for families, and held a "Queer Family Picnic."

We have friends who live in Marietta. We know several couples in Marietta who love Jesus Christ and are raising their families in homes where the Scriptures are central. But our friends now have to defend the well-being of their children. The article goes on to say that similar battles are unfolding in Idaho, Maine, Oregon, Florida, Michigan, Missouri, and Washington. No one is immune to the gay agenda.

When the battle for gay rights comes to your community, gentlemen, I suggest that you be there. This is the only Christian thing for a man to do. This is a battle over the children, and I will address that in just a moment. The homosexual militants play hardball. They loudly condemn the "intolerance" and "hate tactics" of those who oppose them. Yet they are well known for their own confrontational tactics of interrupting church services and threatening those who dare to stand publicly against them.

Because of the tactics of the militant gays, I suggest that this is an issue that requires male leadership. Contrary to popular opinion, real men—especially Christian men—don't send women into combat. When we are surrounded by militant homosexual barbarians who are bent on nothing less than the destruction of every moral load-bearing wall left in this country, then it is the *men* whom God calls to go to battle. That is our situation, gentlemen. I believe that God is looking for men who have such a deep love for Jesus Christ and for their families that they will put themselves on the line. God's men don't put their wives or their kids on the front lines; they put themselves on the line. That's what it's going to take in this assault on morality and godliness.

That's why it's our responsibility, gentlemen, to defend our families from the homosexuals who desire to break down the laws that protect decency and innocence. Martin Luther spoke with a prophetic voice when he said:

If I profess with the loudest voice and clearest exposition every portion of the truth of God except precisely that little point which the world and the Devil are at that moment attacking, I am not confessing Christ, however boldly I may be professing Christ. Where the battle rages, there the loyalty of the soldier is proved, and to be steady on all the battlefield besides, is mere flight and disgrace if he flinches at that point.

Martin Luther rode for the brand. And he is calling us to do the same.

I don't know too many men who relish the idea of getting into a confrontation with a group that throws bricks through windows, leaves butchered animals on doorsteps, paints lewd slogans on the opposition's building, or calls in bomb threats to disrupt the normal activity of those who are willing to stand against them. Focus on the Family experienced all of those things when they supported the 1992 passage of an amendment in Colorado against "protected class" privileges for gays. Dr. James Dobson was the subject of vicious rumors that were pushed without confirmation or hesitation by most of the media.

Why were Jim Dobson and Focus on the Family under attack for taking a moral stand? They were under attack because they had the courage to speak out against a movement that would give homosexuals special rights that no legitimate minority or any other group in this country enjoys. That was the "hate crime" of Focus on the Family.

As for me and my house, we're standing with Focus. And we're standing with them for one reason: They're standing tall.

WHO ARE THEY AND WHAT DO THEY WANT?

Militant homosexuals like to paint themselves as a minority. That is by design. Marshall Kirk and Erastes Pill published an article in the homosexual magazine *Guide* in November 1987. The article, "The Overhauling of Straight America," outlines a strategy by which homosexuals can best implement their agenda. Here are the main points as outlined in the gay strategy:

1. *Desensitization.* "To desensitize the public is to help it view homosexuality with indifference instead of with keen emotion."

2. *Portray gays as victims, not as aggressive challengers.* "In any campaign to win over the public, gays must be cast as victims in need of protection so the straights will be inclined by reflex to assume the role of protector." In other words, make homosexuals a minority.

3. *Give the protectors a just cause.* "Our campaign should not demand direct support for homosexual practices, but instead make anti-discrimination its theme."

4. *Make the victimizers look bad.* "To be blunt—they must be vilified.... The public should be shown images of ranting homophobes whose secondary traits disgust middle America. These images might include the Ku Klux Klan demanding that gays be burned alive or castrated."[59]

Marshall Kirk has one other bit of advice for those trying to elicit sympathy for the plight of the gay movement:

In the early stages of the campaign, the public should not be shocked and repelled by premature exposure to homosexual behavior itself. Instead, the imagery of sex per se should be down-played, and the issue of gay rights reduced as far as possible, to an abstract social question.[60]

A shrewd strategy? You'd better believe it.

A COUNTERSTRATEGY

Part of the problem with this whole issue is that very few people understand the activities of homosexuals. If they did they would get physically ill. Did you notice the suggestions made by the gay activists? In their own words they said that "the public should not be shocked and repelled by premature exposure to homosexual behavior itself." Now why do they stress such a strategy? They stress it because if the public knew what homosexuals did they *would* be shocked and repelled! But that is part of the scam—in other words, if people don't know what homosexuals do, all the while being told that they are a minority and that homosexuality is not a choice but genetic factor, then the homosexual strategists have won the hearts of a lot of people.

That's the strategy. And that's why I want to offer a counterstrategy in the pages that follow.

High noon in America has come and gone. If you've been a casual observer, lying on the tracks and watching the locomotive roll in from a safe distance, you'd better think about taking some action. Bob Dylan used to sing a song about a slow train comin'. This is no slow train, my friend. It's a bullet train.

And it's heading directly your way.

WALKING TALL

1. Read Paul's prophetic words in Romans 1:18–32. Describe the progression (regression?) that begins in verse 18 and ends with the depravity and perversion in verses 24 through 32. With Paul's warnings ringing in your ears, draw parallels with what you see in today's America.

2. In view of Romans 1:18–22, 28–32, discuss this statement: A society that removes prayer, the Ten Commandments, and a belief in the Creator from its schools can expect to reap a deadly harvest in the following generations.

3. Review Leviticus 18:22, 24–30; 20:13. Summarize God's view of homosexual relations, using some of the strong terms that He uses.

4. Take time to again consider Martin Luther's statement, relating it to the militant homosexual's battle for "rights" within your community:

   If I profess with the loudest voice and clearest exposition every portion of the truth of God except precisely that little point which the world and the Devil are at that moment attacking, I am not confessing Christ, however boldly I may be professing Christ. Where the battle rages, there the loyalty of the soldier is proved, and to be steady on all the battlefield besides, is mere flight and disgrace if he flinches at that point.

7

WHEN THE HOUSE
BEGINS TO FALL

GAY WRONGS, PART 1

To the pure, all things are pure,
but to those who are corrupted and
do not believe, nothing is pure.
In fact, both their minds and consciences are corrupted.

TITUS 1:15, NIV

When I finally got my luggage off the carousel, I walked out the glass doors and saw the hotel shuttle pull right up in front of me.

That's what you call timing.

The driver helped haul my stuff on board and we took off for the hotel.

"Ever been to Kansas City before?" he asked.

"No," I replied. "It's my first trip."

The driver then began to tell me a little bit about his town. He was in his fifties and had lived in Kansas City all his life. We continued to talk as the shuttle merged into the exit lane for downtown. That's when I asked a very simple question and got a very unexpected answer.

"How long have you worked at the hotel?"

"Since the first day that it opened in 1980. I've been here the whole time. I was even here the night of the accident."

"Accident? What accident?"

"I was here the night the balconies collapsed. It was the most horrible thing I've ever seen in my life. As long as I live, I'll never be able to get those screams out of my mind. There were people crushed under the weight of the falling balconies—pinned to the floor—but we couldn't get the balconies off of 'em."

And then the man choked up. In the rearview mirror, I could see his eyes welling up with tears. He wasn't able to say anything more for several minutes. Matthys Levy and Mario Salvadori are two structural engineers who describe what the driver of the hotel shuttle was not able to:

> In July 1980 the plushest and most modern hotel in Kansas City, Missouri, the Hyatt Regency, was ready for occupancy after two years of design and two more years of construction....
>
> The Hyatt Regency complex consists of three connected buildings: a slim reinforced concrete tower on the north end, housing the guests' bedrooms and suites; a 117-by-145-foot atrium with a steel and glass roof 50 feet above the floor; and at the south end a four-story reinforced concrete "function," containing all the service areas—meeting rooms, dining rooms, kitchens, etc. The tower was connected to the function block by three pedestrian bridges, or walkways, hung from the steel trusses of the atrium roof: two, one above the other, at the second- and fourth-floor levels near the west side of the atrium and one at the third-floor level near the east side of the atrium. Restaurant service was available at a bar set under the two stacked walkways on the west side of the atrium. The main purpose of the walkways was to permit people to pass between the tower and function block without crossing the often crowded atrium.
>
> At 7:05 P.M. on Friday, July 17, 1981, the atrium was filled with more than sixteen hundred people, most of them dancing to the music of a well-known band for a tea dance competition, when suddenly a frightening, sharp sound like a thunderbolt was heard, stopping the dancers in mid-step. Looking up toward the source of the sound, they

saw two groups of people, on the second and fourth-floor walkways, observing the festivities and stomping in rhythm with the music.

As the two walkways began to fall, the observers were seen holding on to the railings with terrified expressions on their faces. The fourth-floor walkway dropped from the hangers holding it to the roof structure, leaving the hangers dangling like impotent stalactites. Since the second-floor walkway hung from the fourth-floor walkway, the two began to fall together. There was a large roar as the concrete decks of the steel-framed walkways cracked and crashed down, in a billowing cloud of dust, on the crowd gathered around the bar below the second-floor walkway. People were screaming; the west glass wall adjacent to the walkways shattered, sending shards flying over 100 feet; pipes broken by the falling walkways sent jets of water spraying the atrium floor. It was a nightmare the survivors would never forget.... The final count reported 114 dead and over 200 injured, many maimed for life. It was indeed the worst *structural* failure ever to occur in the United States.[61]

It's a tragedy when two balconies holding hundreds of people fall down. It's an even greater tragedy when a nation collapses.

For when a nation collapses, the lives of hundreds of thousands are crushed by tragedy. That's what happened to Israel. Israel collapsed under the weight of Baal worship just as those two balconies at the Hyatt collapsed under the weight of the crowd.

In both cases, the tragedy was the result of a serious, ultimately fatal structural defect.

Fatal Flaws in the Structure

The acceptance and promulgation of homosexuality in a nation is the moral equivalent of a structural defect in a building or a bridge. At a certain point, the weight of the moral wickedness will cause the nation irreparable harm, and the nation will collapse. Dr. Armand Nicholi, eminent psychiatrist and faculty member of the Harvard Medical School, describes the structural problem of a nation that embraces homosexuality:

No society past or present has ever tolerated the institutionalization of homosexuality, for to do so would be to sow the seeds for its own extinction because homosexuality undermines the basic unit of society—the family—and of course precludes procreation, which means extinction of the race.

This is pure common sense. But in America, when the issue of homosexuality comes up, common sense is routinely assassinated.

Solomon had it right when he declared that there is nothing new under the sun. As we view the spiritual deterioration of our nation, we are reminded of the same deterioration that took place in Israel under Ahab and Jezebel. Homosexuality fits into that structural breakdown that was known back then as Baal worship.

Remember the third distinguishing characteristic of Baal worship? Baal worship encouraged and promoted rampant sexual immorality, particularly homosexuality, as a normal and natural alternative lifestyle.

The religion of Baal promoted homosexual activity as part of its worship. It was a religion orchestrated by Satan himself, so it stands to reason that it would violate the holiness and purity of almighty God. There were three kinds of cultic prostitutes in Baalism: male prostitutes, female prostitutes, and sodomite prostitutes. In their public worship and festivals, they would re-create the sexual perversion that is a part of the Baal myths. These public displays were so vile that they cannot be put in print.

The actions of the male sodomite prostitutes of Baal were so filthy that the Hebrew metaphor chosen to describe them was "dog."[62] That's pretty strong language. It's another way of saying their behavior was worse than animals. Why worse? Because animals don't even do the things those guys did.

Now let's be very clear here. Scripture uses the term *dog* to describe the men who were engaged in these activities because what they were doing was an abomination to God. Ahab and Jezebel were not only protecting these prostitutes, but by their association and allegiance with them they were also directly condoning and encouraging such a lifestyle.

The use of the word *abomination* is found 117 times in the Old Testament. The word, which literally means "a detestable thing," has a deep ethical meaning. It covers such topics as witchcraft, sorcery, child sacrifice, and the worship of the sun, moon, and stars. In the Old Testament, the Law demanded death for those who practiced such things. Why? Because God knew that those were the kind of inherent structural defects that would bring down the nation.

A study of the word *abomination* makes it clear that there are some practices, specifically in the context of religion, that God abhors. *These are sins against the person of God Himself.* To understand the sense of the word *abomination*, it is helpful to think of some synonyms. A thesaurus lists words such as *aversion, hate, hatred, loathing, repugnance, horror, repulsion,* and *revulsion.*

We are quickly getting to a point in America where even *speaking* against homosexuality is considered a "hate crime." There are some courts that would have to find God and the Bible guilty, because God says that homosexuality is an abomination.

Abominations are abominations because they are unnatural. They run directly counter to the way God created the world. We are His creation, and He is the ultimate judge of what is natural and what isn't. Our mighty Creator despises sexual perversion and what it does to the souls and lives of those who practice it. To put it plainly, God is strict. He has drawn some very important moral lines. What else would you expect from a perfect heavenly Father?

Does that mean He won't forgive homosexuality? Of course not.

> Or do you not know that the unrighteous shall not inherit the kingdom of God? Do not be deceived; neither fornicators, nor idolaters, nor adulters, nor effeminate, nor homosexuals, nor thieves, nor the covetous, nor drunkards, nor revilers, nor swindlers, shall inherit the kingdom of God. And such were some of you; but you were washed, but you were sanctified, but you were justified in the name of the Lord Jesus Christ, and in the Spirit of our God. (1 Corinthians 6:9–11)

The church is made up of forgiven people. There is no sin that God will not forgive, except the refusal to receive the sacrifice of His Son. But when a person refuses to admit that his behavior is wrong, he embarks on a downward spiral that takes him further and further from the forgiveness of God. That's certainly the message of Romans 1:18–32.

Step One: Suppression of Truth

For the wrath of God is revealed from heaven against all ungodliness and unrighteousness of men, who suppress the truth in unrighteousness, because that which is known about God is evident within them; for God made it evident to them. For since the creation of the world His invisible attributes, His eternal power and divine nature, have been clearly seen, being understood through what has been made, so that they are without excuse. (vv. 18–20)

Step Two: Apathy

For even though they knew God, they did not honor Him as God, or give thanks; but they became futile in their speculations, and their foolish hearts were darkened. Professing to be wise, they became fools, and exchanged the glory of the incorruptible God for an image in the form of corruptible man and of birds and four-footed animals and crawling creatures. (vv. 21–23)

Step Three: Lust

Therefore God gave them over in the lusts of their hearts to impurity, that their bodies might be dishonored among them. For they exchanged the truth of God for a lie, and worshiped and served the creature rather than the Creator, who is blessed forever. Amen. (vv. 24–25)

Step Four: Perversion

For this reason God gave them over to degrading passions; for their women exchanged the natural function for that which is unnatural, and in the same way also the men abandoned the natural function of the women and burned in their desire toward one another, men with men committing indecent acts and receiving in their own persons the due penalty of their error. (vv. 26–27)

Step Five: Depraved Thinking

And just as they did not see fit to acknowledge God any longer, God gave them over to a depraved mind, to do those things which are not proper, being filled with all unrighteousness, wickedness, greed, evil; full of envy, murder, strife, deceit, malice; they are gossips, slanderers, haters of God, insolent, arrogant, boastful, inventors of evil, disobedient to parents, without understanding, untrustworthy, unloving, unmerciful; and, although they know the ordinance of God, that those who practice such things are worthy of death, they not only do the same, but also give hearty approval to those who practice them. (vv. 28–32)

By today's standards, Romans 1 is "intolerant." But that only demonstrates how far we have slid in just over thirty years.

Quite frankly, the militant homosexuals of this new Baal movement are gaining incredible acceptance in our society. And they have an agenda. If environmentalists want the minds of children, homosexuals want the *bodies* of children. Let's look at just who they are.

WHO THEY ARE

Are homosexuals in America in fact a legitimate minority group, disadvantaged and underprivileged? Hardly. As a demographic group:

- the average income for homosexuals is $59,000 per year, versus an annual income of $32,000 for heterosexuals;
- 59.6 percent of homosexuals are college graduates, compared to 18 percent for the national average;
- 49 percent of gays hold professional/managerial positions, compared to 15.9 percent for the national average;
- 26.5 percent are frequent fliers, compared to 1.9 percent of the general population;
- the total homosexual market is estimated to be approximately $400 billion. [63]

This group that is seeking "minority" status is extremely well heeled. They are smart, well financed, and well connected. And, yes, they have an agenda. Homosexuals recruit. They have to recruit. They recruit children and adolescents because they cannot reproduce.

In Boston there is a gay newspaper by the name of the *Gay Community News*. The February 15, 1987, edition contained a lengthy statement by a radical homosexual named Michael Swift. Some have viewed this as the gay rights' Statement of Faith. I have selected the following excerpts:

We shall sodomize your sons, emblems of your feeble masculinity, of your shallow dreams and vulgar lies. We shall seduce them in your schools, in your dormitories, in your gymnasiums, in your locker rooms, in your sports arenas, in your seminaries, in your youth groups, in your movie theater bathrooms, in your army bunkhouses, in your truck stops, in your all-male clubs, in your houses of Congress, wherever men are with men together. Your sons shall become our minions and do our bidding. They will be recast in our image. They will come to crave us and adore us....

All laws banning homosexual activity will be revoked. Instead, legislation shall be passed which engenders love between men....

Homosexuals must stand together as brothers; we must be united artistically, philosophically, socially, politically, and financially. We will triumph only when we present a common face to the vicious heterosexual enemy....

If you dare to cry faggot, fairy, queer at us, we will stab you in your cowardly hearts and defile your dead, puny bodies....

There will be no compromises. We are not middle-class weaklings. Highly intelligent, we're the natural aristocrats of the human race, and steely-minded aristocrats never settle for less. Those who oppose us will be exiled....

The family unit—spawning grounds of lies, betrayals, mediocrity, hypocrisy, and violence—will be abolished. The family unit, which only dampens imagination and curbs free will, must be eliminated. Perfect boys will be conceived and grown in a genetic laboratory. They will be bonded together in a communal setting, under the control and instruction of homosexual savants....

All churches who condemn us will be closed. Our holy gods are handsome young men....

Since we are alienated from middle class heterosexual conventions, we are free to live our lives according to the dictates of pure imagination. For us too much is not enough....[64]

When I read this for the first time, three thoughts came to my mind.

The first was "in your dreams." After I calmed down, the second was that I would like to sit down with the man who wrote this and find out about his relationship with his father. I can assure you that there is a major fissure in this man's life with his dad. The third thought was that this angry and bitter man desperately needs to know Jesus Christ.

Gentlemen, some things are worth fighting for. I had an evangelical pastor tell me last week that he didn't mind if his kids had *seven* homosexual teachers. How tolerant. And how naive. I got the strong sense that this man was not willing to take a stand. He reminded me of a certain Old Testament character named Lot. Lot, you'll remember, got so desensitized to immorality in Sodom that he never did take a stand. As a result, he lost his own family.

God help us if we don't draw the lines *now*. If we don't stand tall as men right now, then the same rights that are being given to homosexuals will soon be given to those who desire to legalize their incest, bestiality, and other unspeakable acts.

It was Blaise Pascal who once said that "those who indulge in perversion tell those who are living normal lives that it is they who are deviating from what is natural." That is the message of the homosexual movement. And it has the fingerprints of Baal all over it.

WHAT THEY WANT

We have just seen that militant homosexuals want access to our children. The question is, how will they obtain that access? The answer is: They must first acquire special rights, which are also known as gay rights.

What are "gay rights"?

Put plainly, gay rights laws are meant to protect men and women who practice oral and anal copulation with members of the same sex. In about half the states, their behavior violates criminal laws.[65]

The test, then, is one of behavior, not status. Homosexuals can be characterized by what they do (sodomy) and with whom they do it (their own sex). According to Magnuson, what gay rights laws ask for is a special privilege for homosexuals not generally available to other groups, such as those who commit incest, bestiality, pedophilia, or, for that matter, any other criminal or antisocial behavior.

Robert Knight, the cultural director of the Family Research Council, describes the gay rights issue with keen insight:

Contrary to their claims of "discrimination," there is no effort to deny homosexuals the same rights guaranteed to all Americans. The truth is that homosexuals have the same rights, with the restrictions, as everyone else. Homosexuals have the right to free speech, freedom of religion, due process under the law, the right to engage in commerce, to enter in contracts, own property, vote, along with a host of other rights. In fact, an ACLU handbook lists dozens of rights homosexuals already enjoy. In this country all citizens are guaranteed equal protection under the law. Homosexuals do not need equal protection.[66]

Despite the fact that homosexuals do not need special rights since they enjoy the same rights as all Americans, they employ militant tactics to obtain their objectives and intimidate their opposition. Militancy is the logo of the gay rights movement. Their modus operandi is to intimidate rather than reason. Magnuson describes the logical consequences of such a militant strategy:

The strategic vision of "total acceptance" articulated by (militant) homosexuals...means public legitimacy, credibility, and community endorsement: in short, making sexual deviance as acceptable as sexual normalcy.[67]

To accomplish that objective, homosexuals now fight tactical battles on three fronts:

1. Where homosexuality is prohibited by law, as in the case of laws prohibiting sodomy, homosexuals seek to repeal those laws or have them declared unconstitutional by the courts.
2. Where there are practices permitted by the law to heterosexuals but not to homosexuals (for example, marriage or adoption of children), homosexuals seek equal privileges for themselves.
3. Where the personal discretion or decision making of individuals impinges on homosexuals—a landlord's choice not to rent to practicing homosexuals, for example—homosexuals seek to pass laws that actually create special privileges for homosexual behavior ("gay rights laws") that are not available for people with more normal behavior.

THE REAL CONSEQUENCES OF GAY RIGHTS

If a gay rights bill or legislation comes to your town (and it inevitably will), then the granting of special rights to homosexuals would also *take* rights from other people in the community—people such as you, your family, and your church. Knight outlines the actual consequences of such legislation:

- Parents would lose the right to protect their children from exposure to homosexuality.
- Private religious and civic groups would no longer be able to exclude homosexuals. Last year the Boy Scouts of America narrowly withstood a challenge from a gay man when the Supreme Court ruled five to four that the Scouts may ban homosexuals from positions as troop leaders. Activists are continuing, however, to pressure the Scouts to change their policies. If such efforts succeed, parents will no longer be free to ensure that organizations to which they entrust their children will convey the parents' values.
- Landlords, even those in duplexes and family-centered complexes, could be forced to rent to open homosexuals.

- Good people of conscience would lose the right to disagree. For example, two Madison, Wisconsin, women were forced to pay fines, attend a political reeducation class, write a letter of apology, and were informed that they were to be monitored by a public agency for two years because they declined to room with a lesbian.[68]

Nothing illustrates the twisted and depraved strategy of the gay rights movement more than their assault on the Boy Scouts. What parents in their right minds would want their son to have a homosexual scoutmaster? Yet such companies as Levi Strauss actually pulled their funding of the Boy Scouts because of the Scouts' refusal to knuckle under to militant homosexual demands. Levi Strauss is one of an increasing number of companies that offer benefits to homosexuals and their "partners" as if they were married couples. Interestingly enough, it pulled its corporate donation to the Boy Scouts about the same time it offered benefits to homosexual couples. As George Grant points out, "Though company representatives insisted their decision was motivated solely by principle, the San Francisco–based company happily admits that 'three out of four gay men prefer Levi's jeans...over other brands.'"[69]

Could that juicy little fact have anything to do with the fact that Levi Strauss thinks that gays should qualify as scoutmasters for the Boy Scouts?

Fortunately, the Boy Scouts have not lost their common sense. They know that many homosexuals would like access to the boys, and some, unfortunately, deceive their way into positions of trust. But at least the Scouts are attempting to keep the barbarians from storming the gates, no thanks to Levi Strauss.

It is an established fact that homosexuality is tied to child molestation.

At least 30 percent of convicted male child molesters have committed homosexual acts and at least 91 percent of those who molested non-familial boys admitted to no sexual contact ever in their lives except with homosexuals.[70]

In France, 129 convicted gays said they had had contact with a total of 11,007 boys (an average of eighty-five per man).[71] Of four hundred consecutive Australian cases of molestation, 64 percent of those assaults were homosexual.[72]

Dr. Paul Cameron has written an excellent pamphlet on this subject. Cameron comments:

> Study after nationwide study has yielded estimates of male homosexuality that range between 1% and 3%. The proportion of lesbians in these studies is almost always lower, usually half that of gays. So, overall, perhaps 2% of adults regularly indulge in homosexuality. Yet, they account for between 20% to 40% of all molestations of children.
>
> Child molestation is not to be taken lightly. Officials at a facility which serves about 1,500 runaway youngsters each year estimate that about half of the boys have been homosexually abused.... Investigation of those suffering chronic mental illness implicates child molestation as a primary cause.
>
> If 2% of the population is responsible for 20% to 40% of something as socially and personally troubling as child molestation, something must be desperately wrong with that 2%. Not every homosexual is a child molester. But enough gays do molest children so that the risk of a homosexual molesting a child is 10 to 20 times greater than that of a heterosexual.[73]

George Grant reports that a recent poll was taken by the National Gay Task Force. The two major priorities of the homosexuals surveyed were the right for admitted homosexuals to be public school teachers and the right of homosexuals to adopt children.[74] They are well on their way to achieving both goals.

Achieving the Unthinkable

This leads us to NAMBLA. That stands for the North American Man/Boy Love Association. This perverse group is taking the philosophy of the homosexual movement to its horrible, yet logical, conclusion. "If there is no such thing as perversion and if sex is good, the exercise of the merely physical appetite, then why should children be denied this good?"[75] Here are some statements from NAMBLA that will make you sick, but gentlemen, we'd better know what these people are up to. They want nothing less than unrestricted access to your children.

NAMBLA takes the view that sex is good, and that homosexuality is good not only for adults, but for young people as well. We support all consensual sexual relationships regardless of age. As long as the relationship is mutually pleasurable and no one's rights are violated, sex should be no one else's business....

Sexual liberation cannot be achieved without the liberation of children. This means many things. Children need to gain control over their lives, a control which they are denied on all sides. They need to break the yoke of "protection" which alienates them from themselves, a "protection" imposed upon them by adults—their family, the schools, the state, and prevailing sexual and social mores....

There is no age at which a person becomes capable of consenting to sex. The age of sexual consent is just one of many ways in which adults impose their system of control of children.[76]

Those statements are nothing less than demonic. Yet I believe that the pressure to endorse homosexuality is so strong in this country that *in the next ten years we will see states begin to either ignore or do away with age-of-consent laws.* In other words, it's just a matter of time before NAMBLA will reach its stated goals.

The only barrier standing in their way is God's men.

May God grant us the courage and strength to stand tall.

BORN TO CHOOSE

A modern piece of propaganda is that homosexuals are born that way. And if they are, then their propensity for children should be excused. Or at least that's the reasoning behind NAMBLA. It seems that every month or so the media reports a study that shows that homosexuality is "genetic." Suffice it to say that you can't believe everything you read in the newspaper. Robert Knight adds a bit of common sense to the equation:

Flawed or misreported science can have enormous political ramifications, as shown by the willingness of the popular journals to tout studies that bolster gay activist views while ignoring others that contradict them. The now-discredited Kinsey-based myth that 10 percent of the population is homosexual is a prime example. Although numerous studies from many nations indicate that the percentages are 2 percent or less, the 10 percent myth lives on.[77]

Knight cites the recent findings of Drs. William Byne and Bruce Parsons who examined past and current claims that homosexuality is genetic. They concluded that "there is no evidence at present to substantiate a biologic theory.... The appeal of current biologic explanations for sexual orientation may derive more from dissatisfaction with the present status of psycho social explanations than from a substantiating body of experimental data."[78] At last, a little bit of common sense from two doctors who are not intimidated by a very powerful group of homosexuals.

Gentlemen, this is a serious threat. Homosexuality has always been around, even when we were children. But the difference now is that homosexuals are attempting to legitimize their access to children through the courts. We cannot sit by and let this happen. For there is an agenda. And it is horrific.

CHURCHES EMBRACING BAAL

Affirmation, Glad, Honesty, Integrity, and Dignity sound like five points you might pick up from a motivational talk on positive thinking. But that's not what they are. These are the names of gay groups lobbying within denominations for acceptance, approval, and sanction. Affirmation is a Methodist group, Glad is with the Disciples of Christ, Honesty is trying to get in with the Southern Baptists, and Integrity is an Episcopalian group.

In addition to these, other gay organizations are American Baptists Concerned (someone needs to start a group called American Baptists Alarmed), the Brethren and Mennonite Council for Lesbian and Gay Concerns, the Presbyterians for Lesbian and Gay Concerns, the Seventh-Day Adventist group by the name of Kinship, and the United Church Coalition for Lesbian and Gay Concerns, which is tied up with the United Church of Christ. The Catholics have two groups bothering them, Dignity and the Catholic Coalition for Gay Civil Rights, while Axios is the gay group in the Greek Orthodox Church.

In addition to these, there are the independent groups working to get into nondenominational evangelical and charismatic churches. I refer to groups such as Evangelicals Concerned, Evangelicals Together, Lambda Christian Fellowship, and the National Gay Pentecostal Alliance. There is also the first gay denomination, the Metropolitan Community Church, which is seeking to join the World Council of Churches.[79]

I would like to offer a suggestion to all of these groups. My suggestion is that they all get together and rent a small banquet room in a hotel (they would only need a small room since all of these groups are very small in number). The purpose of the meeting would be to join together and streamline their efforts. I think they should join together and adopt a common name.

The name that I would like to suggest is "Apostasy."

I think it has a very nice ring to it. Plus, it fits. According to the Oxford English Dictionary, apostasy is "the abandonment or renunciation of one's religious faith or moral allegiance." As the shoe salesmen said to me recently, "If the shoe fits, wear it."

The fourth characteristic of Baal worship is that it attempted to come alongside of Judaism and be regarded as a legitimate part of the worship of Israel. At least that certainly appears to have been the agenda of Jezebel when she married Ahab. That same attempt is being made today in the church of Jesus Christ by homosexual activists.

Obviously today's culture doesn't like this kind of "intolerant" talk. But it's about time somebody stood up and told the truth about this stuff. The militant homosexual rights groups such as Act Up and Queer Nation, and homosexual churches such as the Metropolitan Community Churches and the so-called Cathedral of Hope in Dallas, are the modern-day equivalents of Baal worship. They are tied into the same thinking that brought Baal to Israel...and brought Israel to destruction.

Homosexuality is not a sickness or a disease. It is sinful behavior. Adultery is sinful, alcoholism is sinful, and overeating is sinful. Yet we tend to view all of these as sicknesses. They may be compulsive behaviors, but they are still sin. Each person is still responsible for the choices that he or she makes.

Jay Adams comments:

One is not a homosexual constitutionally any more than one is an adulterer constitutionally. Homosexuality is not considered to be a condition, but an act. It is viewed as a sinful practice which can become a way of life. The homosexual act, like the act of adultery, is the reason for calling one a homosexual. (Of course one may commit homosexual sins of the heart, just as one may commit adultery in his heart. He may lust after a man in his heart as another may lust after a woman).[80]

EVANGELICAL FUDGE

An article a few years ago in *Christianity Today* was entitled "Homosexuality Debate Strains Campus Harmony: Homosexuals at Christian Colleges Press for Acceptance." The lead paragraph of the story was revealing: "Christian college campuses across the country have become the setting for an intense struggle over homosexuality, involving free-speech rights, academic freedom, and theological beliefs."[81]

The article reported on a debate that took place at Calvin College, Eastern College, and Gordon College concerning homosexuality. According to the article, "Four students from Eastern attended the Gay March on Washington in April with a banner proclaiming 'Christian, Gay and Proud—Eastern College Gay and Lesbian Community.'"

The question is this: What is there to debate? The answer is that if one takes a high view of Scripture there is *nothing* to debate.

Dr. Stanton Jones of Wheaton College is exactly right when he says that "the reason homosexuality is an important issue is that what the Bible treats as an isolated act to be condemned—people of the same gender having sex—our society treats as a fundamental element of personal identity."[82] Jones is also dead on target when he makes two other statements. The first is: "Every time homosexual practice is mentioned in the Scriptures, it is condemned."[83] The second is: "There are only two ways one can neutralize the biblical witness against homosexual behavior: by gross misinterpretation or by moving away from a high view of Scripture."[84]

This is the essence of the debates at "Christian" colleges. They are retreating from a high view of Scripture. Lewis Smedes, professor of theology at Fuller Theological Seminary, has also retreated from the scriptural line. In 1976, Smedes wrote a book entitled *Sex for Christians*. In referring to homosexuality, Smedes discusses a concept he calls "creative compassion," for the homosexual who suffers from constitutional homosexuality. This, according to Smedes, is the homosexual who—although responsible for his choices and having gone through therapy—finds that he *cannot* change. The emphasis on *cannot* is pivotal.

As Smedes puts it in his book:

Within his [the homosexual who cannot change] sexual experience, he ought to develop permanent associations with another person, associations in which respect and regard for the other person dominates their sexual relationship.

To develop a morality for the homosexual life is not to accept homosexual practices as morally commendable. It is, however, to recognize that the optimum moral life within a deplorable situation is preferable to a life of sexual chaos.[85]

Teaching that homosexuals cannot change is not only unbiblical, it runs contrary to proven fact.

Dr. Reuben Rine, director of the New York Center for Psychoanalytic Training, has found that almost any program will be successful when it is dedi-cated to helping homosexuals who wish to get out of the lifestyle. Many people have, indeed, given up homosexuality under all kinds of treatment programs. "The misinformation that homosexuality is untreatable by psychotherapy does incalculable harm to thousands of men and women."[86]

If psychotherapy can help change homosexuality, certainly the Word of God can, too.

To further drive home the point that homosexuals can indeed change, Dr. Joseph Nicolosi has written a book entitled *Reparative Therapy of Male Homosexuality*. It's the kind of book to keep on the bedstand for some light reading before you fall off to sleep (just kidding). Allow me to sum up Dr. Nicolosi's theory, for it is critical to this concession that so many Christians are making that homosexuals "cannot" change their behavior. Nicolosi's counseling technique is based on:

> ...a developmental view that the homosexual condition is the result of incomplete gender-identity development arising when there is conflict and subsequent distancing from the father. This defensive detachment is the psychological mechanism by which the prehomosexual boy removes himself emotionally from the father (or father figure) and fails to establish a male identity. Many homosexuals are attracted to other men because they are striving to complete their own gender-identification.[87]

Nicolosi's basic thesis is that homosexuals have been emotionally cut off from proper identification and relationship with their fathers. It is a condition that, once understood, can be repaired through *rightly* relating emotionally to other men or father figures. Nicolosi has had unusual success with homosexual men who *have changed* their identity and behavior. The reason I am quoting these two psychologists is that if there are psychologists who are saying that homosexuality is a behavior that *can* be changed, then it is a tragedy when those in the church say that it *cannot* be changed. The reason it is a tragedy is that the Scriptures clearly state that homosexuals can change (1 Corinthians 6:9–11).

Smedes is to be commended for his desire to express compassion to the person who is struggling with homosexuality. But the kind of compassion that people need is not creative compassion but *biblical* compassion. In his attempt to extend compassion, what Smedes has done is to grant permission for someone to continue in a type of sexual conduct that the Bible expressly forbids. That, ultimately, is not compassion. Jesus made it clear to His disciples that if they were to be His disciples, then they were to abide in His Word, and the truth would set them free (John 8:31–32).

Compassion without truth sets no one free. And advancing the myth that homosexuals cannot change simply gives permission to practice a behavior that the Scriptures clearly condemn.

One of the leading spokesmen for the gay rights agenda is Dr. Mel White. White is a former professor from Fuller Theological Seminary. In fact, he taught there when Smedes released his book. White now calls himself a gay Christian and is "justice minister" for a large gay church in Dallas. According to the *Dallas Morning News*, Mel White came out of the closet in the early 1980s.[88] He divorced his wife of twenty-two years and left her and their two children for the homosexual life. I recently saw Mel White on the *Larry King Live*. Time and time again, he alluded to his sexuality as something that one "cannot" change.

When I first read of Mel White's decision to pursue the gay lifestyle, the thought that came to my mind was Lewis Smedes's book. In his book, Smedes opened the door, and Mel White walked through it. Smedes's "creative compassion" was wrong in 1976, and it's wrong today. But it is definitely gaining acceptance in evangelical churches where the lines are being moved to stay in step with a culture that is marching to the drumbeat of Baal.

Rechalking the Field

Why have I written two chapters on this topic?

One reason. Our children are at risk.

Yes, homosexuality has always been around. But it has not always demanded authentication and acceptance from the rest of society as the movement is now doing. They are not content just to have their own neighborhoods and sections of a city. They want in the schools. They want to adopt kids. And they want special rights. For now, the churches and Christian schools will be exempt. For now. But we are kidding ourselves to think those exemptions will last.

Men, it's time to draw a line, and draw it right here.

When this issue comes up at a school board meeting, *be there.*

When a gay rights bill comes before your city council, *be there.*

Don't send your wife while you stay home to watch the ball game. You go to the meeting. Go prepared, and don't go alone. Take some guys with you and pray for one another during the meeting.

I opened this discussion in the last chapter by referring to the shift that *Time* magazine made in its acceptance of homosexuality in 1968. Let me relate something that happened to me at the airport. Before boarding a flight from

Chicago to Portland, I picked up the latest *Time* at the newsstand. As I flipped through the issue I came across an article titled, "For the Love of Kids: What Should Be Done with a Teacher Who Belongs to a Pedophile Group but Has a Spotless Record?"[89]

The article is about a New York City schoolteacher who is also a member of NAMBLA. I must tell you that this article will be as significant to the acceptance of pedophiles as the *Time* article of 1968 was to homosexuals. While the magazine does not condone his behavior, they do paint him as an innocent victim. This is the first "pedophile victim" story I've ever seen in a major newsmagazine. Mark my words, guys, it's just the first of many. The opening paragraphs of the article are classics:

> The principle behind a legal defense based on civil liberty is often illustrated by the famous lament of a Dachau prisoner: "They came first for the communists, and I didn't speak up because I wasn't a communist. Then they came next for the Jews, and I didn't speak up because I wasn't a Jew." And so on, through the trade unionists and the Catholics, until, "Then they came for me, and by that time no one was left to speak up."
>
> The question in the case of New York City teacher Peter Melzer is, "Is it possible, in all sincerity, to begin that recitation, 'They came for the pedophiles...'?"[90]

Gentlemen, this bullet train has just sped up. What should be done with a teacher who belongs to a pedophile group but has a spotless record? Most people will tell you what should be done—because they still have a line or two they're willing to stand behind. And one of those lines is sex with children. But that line is going to be challenged just as the homosexual line was challenged and erased twenty years ago.

Are you ready to draw the line? Are you willing to say, "It's here and no further"?

If godly men won't draw it, then who will?

The answer is that *no one* will.

But you and I will show up at the school board meeting. We'll show up at the city council meeting. We'll square our shoulders, stand tall, and take the heat. And we will also fast and pray, because this battle is ultimately a spiritual one.

But one thing is for sure: We will *not* retreat.

We *will* protect our children.

And we will do it because we're ridin' for the brand.

WALKING TALL

1. Allow me to put a reverse spin on an old football cliché and say, *The best defense is a good offense.* As you consider the powerful, mysterious words of Paul in Ephesians 5:22–33, describe how biblically obedient, Christ-centered marriages can turn back the creeping shadows of depravity and perversion in our country.

2. As you continue to reflect on the above passage, why does the Lord place so much importance on the "object lesson" of a loving husband and wife living together in sexual purity? Why does the perversion of that divinely ordained model cause the Lord so much grief and righteous anger?

3. It's very easy to read a chapter like this and become "worked up." That's not so bad. A lot of us need to be worked up over what's happening in our country. But as men who ride for the Lord Jesus, we need to display the kind of balance that He displayed when faced with a hostile, hateful world. Compare His reactions to the following situations:

    Jesus in the temple (John 2:13–17).
    Jesus at the feast (John 7:30–38).
    Jesus approaches Jerusalem (Luke 13:34–35; 19:41–44).
    Jesus with the teachers and Pharisees (Matthew 23:13–36).
    Jesus with the crowds (Matthew 9:36; 11:28–30).

    How can we bring that kind of balance to our struggle with epidemic immorality and perversion in our country?

8

ELIJAH
STANDS TALL

Tolerance is the virtue of people
who don't believe in anything.
G. K. CHESTERTON

Orestes Lorenzo Perez loved his country, but he couldn't stomach what was happening in it.

So in March of 1991, Lorenzo got into his MiG-23 fighter jet, flew it under U.S. radar, and safely landed in Key West, Florida. Upon defecting, he figured that Castro, embarrassed to have one of his top pilots defect, would immediately release Lorenzo's wife and his young sons to join him.

Lorenzo was wrong.

But Lorenzo wasn't through.

For the next twenty-one months, Lorenzo spent every waking hour trying to get his family out. After months of frustration, Lorenzo decided on a plan that was crazy. He decided that his only chance was to fly back to Cuba and get his family. Only this time he didn't have a jet. He had a little thirty-one-year-old Cessna.

On December 19, 1992, at 5:05 P.M., Lorenzo took off from Florida for a little seaside village in Cuba. He had been able to smuggle a message to his wife to tell her of the plan. But his chances of getting through the net of radar and MiGs that surrounded Cuba were slim and none. If he was spotted, it would be over in an instant. So he flew in just as he had flown out, skimming scant inches over the waves.

At 5:43 P.M. his wife, Victoria, spotted the plane as he was attempting to land on the busy highway just two blocks from the beach. She grabbed her boys and they started running.

Lorenzo brought the little Cessna down on the highway, narrowly missing a boulder in the middle of the road. Then he pulled to a stop just ten yards short of a head-on collision with a wide-eyed truck driver.

Lorenzo says that the hardest part (and the part that still pains him) was when Victoria and the boys jumped in—and he didn't even have time to hug or kiss them.

"Shut up and sit down!" he yelled. "I have to fly the plane!"

They hit American airspace twenty-one minutes later, and that's when the hugs and kisses began.

The night before he took off, Lorenzo was praying in a small chapel. A woman came up to him and said, "Don't be afraid. Your trip will be a success." Lorenzo didn't know this woman and immediately wondered how she could know of his plans for the next day. He could only believe that God was speaking to him, assuring him that he would not be flying alone.[91]

There can be no doubt that Orestes Lorenzo Perez is a man of courage, conviction, and character. He's a man who stands tall.

You might say that he's flyin' for the brand.

ANOTHER TIME AND ANOTHER PLACE

Elijah loved his country, but he couldn't stomach what was happening in it.

So Elijah decided to take a little trip to Samaria to speak directly to King Ahab. We don't know how he got there, and we don't know how he got past the guards to see the king. Elijah had a way of just showing up. And Ahab had to be as shocked to see Elijah as that truck driver was to see Lorenzo.

You see, God had had it with Ahab and Baal worship. It was killing the nation of Israel, God's chosen nation. Ahab was bringing Israel down like those balconies came down in Kansas City. So God looked for a man that he could trust to deliver a message to Ahab.

> Now Elijah the Tishbite, from Tishbe in Gilead, said to Ahab, "As the LORD, the God of Israel, lives, whom I serve, there will be neither dew nor rain in the next few years except at my word." (1 Kings 17:1, NIV)

Elijah was pretty direct. With that brief announcement to Ahab, he had fired off a direct challenge to this false god, Baal, who was bringing down the entire nation.

Why was it a direct challenge to Baal? Because they all thought Baal controlled the rain. Oswald Sanders nails it down for us when he writes, "Baal was a god of many faces—being a god of rain, fertility, and the personification of the sun."[92] A common name for Baal was "The Rider of the Clouds." It was Baal who supposedly determined when and where the rain would fall.

Elijah looked around and saw that Israel was falling apart. He saw the immorality and apostasy. He saw Ahab and Jezebel and their troop of 850 prophets. And he saw that their belief system was destroying the moral and spiritual infrastructure of the nation. He also saw that they played hardball. They had killed the other prophets who had stood up to them. They had killed so many that Elijah legitimately thought he was the only one left. So what did Elijah do in the midst of those overwhelming odds?

Did he retreat?

No.

He stood tall and spoke the truth. No matter what the outcome, no matter what the cost, no matter what the odds against him, he took a stand. He was not going to let the moral erosion continue unchecked. Matthew Henry summarizes the situation:

> Never was Israel so blessed with a good prophet as when it was so plagued with a bad king. Never was a king so bold to sin as Ahab, never was a prophet so bold to reprove and threaten as Elijah.... He

only, of all the prophets, had the honor of Enoch, the first prophet, to be translated, that he should not see death, and the honor of Moses, the great prophet, to attend our Savior in his transfiguration. Other prophets prophesied and wrote, he prophesied and acted, but wrote nothing; but his actions cast more luster on his name than their writings did on theirs.[93]

Now remember, Ahab was the king of *Israel*. Israel wasn't just any nation; it was God's nation. These were God's people who had been called for a specific purpose. They were to be distinct and different because God has something very special for them to accomplish as a nation in His plan for the world.

The problem was the rule of Ahab and Jezebel. They thought Israel belonged to them. They were having a great time leading the nation down a path of godlessness, immorality, and wickedness. And they were getting away with it, or so it seemed, until Elijah showed up.

Who was Elijah? Quite simply, Elijah was a man who couldn't be bought. You've heard it said that every man has his price? Not Elijah. Elijah was sold out 100 percent to the God of Israel, Yahweh. Elijah was ridin' for the brand.

Elijah showed up and did something that was very, very foreign to Ahab and Jezebel.

He told the truth.

You see, Elijah had no interest in public opinion polls. The leather-clad prophet from the backcountry of Gilead had no inclination to please special interest groups. Elijah was not one to make promises to any audience for any reason, just to secure their support. Elijah wasn't a politician. Elijah was a prophet. That simply means that he spoke the Word of God. Period.

It didn't matter what it was that God wanted him to say.

If it was politically incorrect, he said it.

If it was unpopular, he said it.

If it was offensive, he said it.

If people didn't understand, he said it.

If people were going to ridicule him and talk behind his back, he said it.

Elijah spoke the truth of God.

As suddenly as Elijah showed up, he left. He was gone for three years. Elijah might have left, but his message didn't. Not a single drop of rain dared to hit the ground after Elijah, the servant of God, had spoken. This was all painfully clear to Ahab and Jezebel.

Gentlemen, what Elijah did took tremendous courage. Elijah faced Ahab by himself. A lesser man would have worried about the possibility of losing his life after speaking so directly to a king. But not Elijah. Elijah was a man of courage. He delivered the message and then:

> The word of the LORD came to him, saying, "Go away from here and turn eastward, and hide yourself by the brook Cherith, which is east of the Jordan. And it shall be that you shall drink of the brook, and I have commanded the ravens to provide for you there." So he went and did according to the word of the LORD, for he went and lived by the brook Cherith, which is east of the Jordan. And the ravens brought him bread and meat in the morning and bread and meat in the evening, and he would drink from the brook. (1 Kings 17:2–6)

There is a very simple reason God told Elijah to go to Cherith. It was for his protection. As the weeks and months went by, and no rain appeared, Ahab got hotter and hotter (no pun intended). The reality of Elijah's prophecy began to hit home. Baal or no Baal, it really wasn't going to rain until Elijah said so. If Ahab was angry, Jezebel must have been livid. For she was the one who had brought Baal with her when she married Ahab. And it was Jezebel who really ran the show. As several commentators have pointed out, she ruled Ahab, therefore she ruled the nation.

The name Jezebel means "unmarried" or "without cohabitation."[94] As one reads the pages of the Old Testament, it becomes quite clear that the marriage of Ahab and Jezebel was nothing more than a clever political alliance. When two people of such character deficit as Ahab and Jezebel get together in marriage, the focus isn't intimacy and romance; it's naked ambition and raw power.

J. Vernon McGee described Jezebel as "a masculine woman with strong intellectual powers and a fierce passion for evil. She was strong-willed and possessed a dominant personality, but she had no moral sense. She was hardened into insensibility. She was unscrupulous and the most wicked person in history—bar none."[95] Those are pretty strong words. They also happen to be right on track. In Revelation 2:20, Jesus spoke to the church at Thyatira:

I have this against you, that you tolerate the woman Jezebel, who calls herself a prophetess, and she teaches and leads My bond-servants astray, so that they commit acts of immorality and eat things sacrificed to idols.

Why would two people such as Ahab and Jezebel ever let Elijah out of the palace alive? I think that they must have been so surprised by his entrance and so stunned by his boldness that they didn't know what hit them. He delivered his message and then in the silence following that prophetic concussion bomb, he was gone. You can put your money on the fact that a likeness of the prophet's mug soon graced every post office across Israel. As far as Ahab and Jezebel were concerned, he was "most wanted." The Scriptures indicate that there was not a nation or kingdom where Ahab didn't look for Elijah (1 Kings 18:10).

There is much speculation about the location of Cherith, but frankly, no one knows for sure where it was. More importantly, Ahab didn't know where it was. We don't know *where* it was, but we do know *what* it was: It was a place of protection where God took care of Elijah's needs.

Sometimes we are hesitant to speak out when we should. In our hearts, we know that we should, but we are reluctant because it might cost us something to do so. The story of Elijah reminds us that God is our protector. He has a way of looking out for those who are willing to stand tall and speak out for truth. God has ways of protecting us and our families that we would never dream of. One man experienced that protection in a most extraordinary way.

Elmer Bendiner flew numerous bombing runs over Germany in World War II. In his book *The Fall of the Fortresses*, he recalls one bombing run that he will never forget.

Our B-17 [*The Tondelayo*] was barraged by flak from Nazi antiaircraft guns. That was not unusual, but on this particular occasion our gas tanks were hit. Later, as I reflected on the miracle of a twenty-millimeter shell piercing the fuel tank without touching off an explosion, our pilot, Bohn Fawkes, told me it was not quite that simple.

On the morning following the raid, Bohn had gone down to ask our crew chief for that shell as a souvenir of unbelievable luck. The crew chief told Bohn that not just one shell but eleven had been found in the gas tanks—eleven unexploded shells where only one was sufficient to blast us out of the sky. It was as if the sea had parted for us. Even after thirty-five years, so awesome an event leaves me shaken, especially after I heard the rest of the story from Bohn.

He was told that the shells had been sent to the armorers to be defused. The armorers told him that Intelligence had picked them up. They could not say why at the time, but Bohn eventually sought out the answer.

Apparently, when the armorers opened each of those shells, they found no explosive charge. They were clean as a whistle and just as harmless. Empty? Not all of them.

One contained a carefully rolled piece of paper. On it was a scrawl in Czech. The Intelligence people scoured our base for a man who could read Czech. Eventually, they found one to decipher the note. It set us marveling. Translated, the note read: "This is all we can do for you now."[96]

Perhaps the idea of taking a stand on the issue of homosexuality is more than you can handle. Or it may be taking a stand at your office or your place of employment. We tend to worry about what might happen if we take a stand for the Lord. The Lord has promised to protect us just as He did Elijah. He knows how to get us to a brook where our needs will be met, and He knows how to keep our enemies from finding us.

A little lady by the name of Amy Carmichael spent her life spreading the gospel in India. She became aware of a horrible practice that was common at the Hindu temples. Little girls as young as six and seven would be sold by their parents into lives of prostitution. Amy Carmichael could not bear the thought of such brutality to little girls. So she decided to do something about it.

Through miraculous means, the first little girl was brought to her in 1901. The little seven-year-old girl showed Amy her hands, which had been branded with hot irons because she had tried to escape. By 1943, Amy was taking care of nearly eight hundred children, and she was despised by a powerful system of prostitution that been in effect for nearly a thousand years. But God protected this woman who had the courage to stand for the Word of God. Gentlemen, if God could protect Amy Carmichael all of those years, then we should ask God to give us just a tenth of her courage.

MAN OF CONVICTION, MAN OF COMPROMISE

It would be easy to spend an entire book on the life of Elijah. Since we can't do that, let's jump nearly three years ahead when Elijah shows himself again to Ahab.

> Now it came after many days, that the word of the LORD came to Elijah in the third year, saying, "Go, show yourself to Ahab, and I will send rain on the face of the earth." So Elijah went to show himself to Ahab. Now the famine was severe in Samaria. And Ahab called Obadiah who was over the household. (Now Obadiah feared the LORD greatly; for it came about, when Jezebel destroyed the prophets of the LORD, that Obadiah took a hundred prophets and hid them by fifties in a cave, and provided them with bread and water.) Then Ahab said to Obadiah, "Go through the land to all the springs of water and to all the valleys; perhaps we will find grass and keep the horses and mules alive, and not have to kill some of the cattle." So they divided the land between them to survey it; Ahab went one way by himself and Obadiah went another way by himself.
>
> Now as Obadiah was on the way, behold, Elijah met him, and he recognized him and fell on his face and said, "Is this you, Elijah my master?" And he said to him, "It is I. Go, say to your master, 'Behold, Elijah is here.' " And he said, "What sin have I committed, that you are giving your servant into the hand of Ahab, to put me to death? As the LORD your God lives, there is no nation or kingdom where my master has not sent to search for you; and when they said, 'He is not here,' he made the kingdom or nation swear that they could not find you. And now you are saying, 'Go, say to your master, "Behold, Elijah is here." ' And it will come about when I leave you that the Spirit of the LORD will carry you where I do not know; so when I come and tell Ahab and he cannot find you, he will kill me, although I your servant have feared the LORD from my youth. Has it not been told to my master what I did when Jezebel killed the prophets of the LORD, that I hid a hundred prophets of the LORD by fifties in a cave, and provided them with bread and water? And now you are saying 'Go, say to your master, "Behold, Elijah is here" '; he will then kill me." And Elijah said,

"As the LORD of hosts lives, before whom I stand, I will surely show myself to him today."

So Obadiah went to meet Ahab and told him; and Ahab went to meet Elijah. (1 Kings 18:1–16)

This dialogue between Elijah and Obadiah is critical. As we know, Elijah is a man of courage, conviction, and character. I want to suggest to you that Obadiah, although the text states very clearly that he is a believer, is a weak man in contrast to Elijah. Obadiah is a picture of compromise. Instead of courage, conviction, and character, he demonstrates cold feet, compromise, and convenience.

Elijah	*Obadiah*
courage	cold feet
conviction	compromise
character	convenience

Warren Wiersbe has noted some rather marked differences between Elijah and Obadiah:

Elijah was serving the Lord publicly and without fear; Obadiah was serving Ahab and trying to serve the Lord secretly. Elijah was "outside the camp" (Hebrews 13:13); Obadiah was inside the court. Elijah knew the will of God; Obadiah did not know what was going on. While Elijah was laboring to save the nation, Obadiah was out looking for grass to save the horse and mules. When Elijah confronted Obadiah, the frightened servant did not trust the prophet. And note that Obadiah had to "brag" about his secret service to impress Elijah with his devotion.[97]

THE QUESTION OF LEADERSHIP

There's an age-old question about leaders. Are they born or are they made? All leaders must be born...and from there they are constantly learning.

I believe that what is going to be required for this new era of American history is two things: courage and holiness. That's why some of you who are reading this are going through such difficult experiences in your personal lives right now. God is getting you ready for leadership. God is preparing His men and women to take a moral stand for Christ in a generation that is becoming increasingly hostile to the gospel.

"Wait a minute!" you may be saying. "I'm not a leader. And I'm not sure I have what it takes to be a leader in that kind of climate."

Sure you do. I recently came across what I consider to be a very insightful column on leadership. It was written to business entrepreneurs, but I think the parallels to our discussion will be quite clear. Wilson L. Harrell writes:

Psychologists claim that leadership asserts itself early in life. They're wrong. How many voted "most likely to succeed" at your school ever amounted to anything? Leadership is acquired—forged in the hell of combat. Being called upon to "face fire" transmutes ordinary men into leaders. It matters not whether the bullets are the lead kind or the more insidious projectiles of corporate battle.

A few years after every war, there is an explosion of entrepreneurship. Why? Because many of us discover courage we never knew we had. Courage is the kernel of leadership. In World War II, I was a combat fighter pilot flying a P38, giving "close support" to General Patton in his march through France. Our mission was to bomb and strafe enemy positions ahead of his troops. One day, my flight of four planes was ordered to take out a German airfield 100 miles behind their lines. We zoomed down, made our run, and survived the anti-aircraft fire. As we pulled up, I saw in the distance what looked like a big flock of buzzards. Then I realized: "Those aren't buzzards. Those are airplanes...German airplanes!"

I got on the intercom and called in to my leader, Jerry Gardner. In a voice two octaves above high C, I yelled: "Jerry, there's a whole mess of bogeys at 10 o'clock low!" Jerry looked up. After a moment of silence, he said calmly, "Let's go get 'em."

Off we went, four idiots chasing what turned out to be 67 enemy fighters—the dreaded Hermann Goering yellow-nose fighters. Toward the end of the war, America had destroyed most of the

Luftwaffe, so General Goering brought together his best pilots into one invincible unit. They'd had a field day bombing our airfields and killing our troops. They'd never been challenged—until now.

As we got closer, we could see that they carried bombs and belly tanks. They were off bombing some unsuspecting airfield and not eager to play with the four of us. Then they turned into us—67 of them head-on. Almost in range. My backside was chewing up the seat. Now, there is one sacred rule in the Air Force: Always keep formation. The only way to survive air-to-air combat is to stay together and protect each other. At that moment, Jerry got on the horn and uttered some immortal words:

"Every man for himself."

We zoomed right into the middle of their formation. I ended up on the tail of a German general leading the group with his three wingmen. Nobody behind me could shoot at me for fear of hitting the general—a no-no for any German pilot who didn't want to face a firing squad. I shot down the three wingmen without even getting shot at.

Then the general and I had ourselves [a terrifying] dogfight. He probably flew into my fire, since from the beginning I was squeezing every trigger in the cockpit. He went down.

The next second, every [enemy fighter] that wasn't shooting at Jerry and my other two buddies opened up on me. My plane and I caught fire.

I bailed out, pulled my rip cord, and looked up. My chute was on fire.... Luckily, I was so low that my chute swung only a couple of times before I hit the ground, badly burned, and was picked up by the French underground. Eleven days later, when I was near death, Patton sent in a squadron of tanks to get me out of there.

The day of our dogfight, 47 yellow-nose fighters were shot down.... All four of us survived and earned Presidential citations. But the real question is: Why? Why did three pilots willingly follow Jerry into what we knew was most certain death?

Jerry Gardner was a leader. Remembering his example, I became one.[98]

That's precisely why we are looking at the example of Elijah. That's why I would suggest that you take some time and read the entire scriptural account of the life of Elijah. It really doesn't take that long to get through his biography. You start in 1 Kings 17 and read through 2 Kings 2:14. That's a total of about seven chapters. And in those seven chapters you'll see firsthand the example of Elijah's leadership.

Elijah wasn't perfect. There was a brief time after his mighty victory over the four hundred prophets of Baal that he lost perspective. That often happens after a great victory. It's following a great triumph that a man is most susceptible to depression. And that's what happened to Elijah. As James tells us, "Elijah was a man with a nature like ours" (James 5:17).

But the clear and steady evidence shows Elijah to be a man of courage, conviction, and character. Obadiah, on the other hand, was a man who tried to play both ends against the middle. And that is the road to ruin.

Quite frankly, Obadiah is a puzzle to me. He also puzzles Old Testament commentators. Obadiah is a mystery because he demonstrated behaviors that are contradictory. On one hand he appeared to be committed, but on the other…what was he doing *working for Ahab?* Someone recently reminded me that Daniel, too, worked in a high government position for pagan kings. So what was wrong with Obadiah being in that position?

Nothing was wrong with him having the position. What was wrong was that he *held on* to the position instead of standing up to Ahab.

It's apparent from Obadiah's conversation with Elijah that Obadiah was more concerned about saving his life than he was about speaking the truth. Daniel would never have done that. Daniel never compromised his faith, that's why he spent some time at the lion exhibit in the Babylon zoo. Think about Shadrach, Meshach, and Abednego. They were willing to walk into the fire rather than compromise their convictions. But Obadiah was trying to play both sides. And that was his problem. Obadiah was a believer, and he had convictions. His problem was that he was way too willing to compromise those convictions in ways that Daniel, Shadrach, Meshach, and Abednego never would have.

Obadiah was a compromiser. Elijah told it straight and took the heat. Obadiah had a great job that was hard to give up. Elijah lived day to day in complete dependence on the Holy One of Israel. Obadiah was part of a group that promoted wickedness, killing, and immorality—although he himself found those things to be wrong.

The problem with Obadiah was that he was like a chameleon. A chameleon is a small lizard that can change colors to fit into its environment. Our colors should be true.

I walked into my study one morning and found some text on my desk. My daughter had made copies of a quote for her high school Bible study and had inadvertently left one on my desk. It makes the point about as clearly as it can be made. Seattle pastor Bob Moorehead wrote these words, and I find them well worth repeating:

I am part of the Fellowship of the Unashamed. I have the Holy Spirit's power. The die has been cast. I have stepped over the line. The decision has been made. I am a disciple of Jesus Christ. I won't look up, let up, slow down, back away, or be still. My past is redeemed, my present makes sense, and my future is secure. I am finished and done with low living, sight walking, small planning, smooth knees, colorless dreams, tame visions, mundane talking, chintzy giving, and dwarfed goals.

I no longer need pre-eminence, prosperity, position, promotions, plaudits, or popularity. I don't have to be right, first, tops, recognized, praised, regarded, or rewarded. I now live by presence, lean by faith, love by patience, lift by prayer, and labor by power. My pace is set, my gait is fast, my goal is heaven, my road is narrow, my way is rough, my companions few, my guide reliable, my mission clear. I cannot be bought, compromised, deterred, lured away, turned back, diluted, or delayed. I will not flinch in the face of sacrifice, hesitate in the presence of adversity, negotiate at the table of the enemy, ponder at the pool of popularity, or meander in the maze of mediocrity. I won't give up, back up, let up, or shut up until I've preached up, prayed up, stored up, and stayed up the cause of Christ.

I am a disciple of Jesus Christ. I must go until Heaven returns, give until I drop, preach until all know, and work until He comes. And when He comes to get His own, He will have no problem recognizing me. My colors will be clear.

The author of this statement is ridin' for the brand. Elijah would have signed off on this, too, because he was also ridin' for the brand. But Obadiah…well, Obadiah was just ridin'. Sometimes he was riding for the brand and other times he was just riding. In other words, Obadiah's colors weren't always clear. But they needed to be. What a pity it is that I know some high school girls who are more willing than their fathers to let their colors be clear. What those girls need are dads who are willing to stand tall.

How about your colors? Are they clear or are they muddled? Are your colors clear in your career? Are they clear with your kids? Are they clear with the IRS? Are they clear when it comes to sexual purity? Are you ridin' for the brand, or are you just ridin'? Are you standing tall, or just standing around?

To put it in a nutshell, guys, I believe every Christian family needs a man of courage, character, and guts at the helm. A man willing to stand tall no matter what. That's the kind of leadership it's going to take to lead a family in a culture that is becoming more and more hostile to Christianity every day. These are times of great necessities and great pressure for God's people. That's why God is looking for His men to step up to the plate and be great leaders.

Great and extraordinary undertakings require character, conviction, and courage. Louis Adamic wrote: "There is a certain blend of courage, integrity, character, and principle which has no satisfactory dictionary name but has been called different things at different times in different countries." Our American name for it is "guts." Elijah had guts. And so did Peter Cartwright.

Peter Cartwright was a circuit-ridin' Methodist preacher back in the nineteenth century. He stood tall, he shot straight, and he rode for the brand. On one occasion Cartwright was getting ready to preach to a very large congregation when he was told that President Andrew Jackson would be in the audience. His friends, who knew Mr. Cartwright well, asked him to make sure that his remarks were positive and inoffensive.

Peter Cartwright preached his sermon. Somewhere in that sermon he said, "I have been told that Andrew Jackson is in this congregation. And I have been asked to guard my remarks. What I must say is that *Andrew Jackson will go to hell* if he doesn't repent of his sin."

The congregation, of course, was aghast. Yet after the service, President Jackson made his way to Peter Cartwright and extended his hand.

"Sir," the president said, "if I had a regiment of men like you, I could whip the world."

Do you know what I think? I think God is looking for some Peter Cartwrights today. I think He's scanning the horizon for an Elijah or two. I think He is looking for some men who have a great love for Jesus Christ and a great love for their families and a great love for this nation. The light in America has grown dim, but the light is still on. I don't know of too many guys who climb into a Cessna in Havana and land on a road in Florida to rescue their families and then hightail it back to Cuba. America is not what it used to be morally or spiritually, but the light is still on, and it still beats the alternative.

But if the light is going to *remain* on and if—in God's great grace—the light is going to get stronger, then you can count on the fact that God will work through His men to lead the charge.

Men who love Jesus Christ more than they love personal peace.

Men who love their families more than they love their comfort.

Men who love holiness more than they love popularity.

Men who love their country enough to get on their knees to ask God to bring a genuine revival to this nation.

Men who are willing to go to battle to protect their families and save their nation.

Are you willing to put yourself on the line? Are you willing to even put your job on the line? If you're not, then do yourself a favor and stop reading this book right now. But if you are willing to go to battle, if you are willing to stand up and speak the truth, if you are willing to be persecuted, if necessary, for righteousness' sake, then read on. You're ridin' for the brand.

The great comedian of old movies, W. C. Fields, once said, "A dead fish can float downstream, but it takes a live one to swim against the current." The easy thing is to float. It's tough, especially in this culture, to swim against the current. But that's exactly what it's going to take.

We're raising our children at a time when many of our nation's leaders have more in common with the Baal-worshiping kings of the Old Testament than with our founding fathers. These leaders are fundamentally opposed to the moral absolutes upon which this country was founded.

So what is our response to all of this? To be more specific, what is your response going to be?

One option is to do nothing. Just raise our hands in disgust and become reconciled to the fact that there is nothing we can do to stem the tide. But I don't think that's the correct response. Elijah certainly didn't do that. Elijah got involved. You might even say that he got involved politically, since he personally confronted the king.

If you are a Christian father and husband, then you are salt and you are light. And if salt and light don't start making appearances all over this country, then we can go ahead and just hand over the key to our cities and towns to the new Baal worshipers.

Some will say that we shouldn't get involved in politics or in school boards. The liberals are definitely saying that, but unfortunately, there are some Christians saying the same thing. Christians shouldn't be involved in politics, because politics are "worldly."

I must heartily disagree. The fact of the matter is this: The political issues of our day, issues such as homosexual rights, abortion rights, sex education in the classroom, and values clarification in the classroom, *are at their core not political issues* but spiritual issues. I read somewhere that we are to be in the world but not of the world. Therefore we cannot retreat, because the future of our children and their children are on the line. That's why Orestes Lorenzo Perez was willing to put it all on the line.

Guys, are you willing to put it all on the line? To be a man who loves his wife, who isn't going to flake out and pursue another woman, who won't be afraid to take a stand in his community on moral issues, who isn't reading public opinion polls to find out where he should stand, who will turn off the TV and read the Bible to his kids?

Gentlemen, God always has His Elijahs. God always has His men. Are you going to be an Elijah or an Obadiah?

The King of kings awaits your answer.

WALKING TALL

1. Elijah wasn't afraid to take on the political powers that be in an Israel that had tossed aside its godly heritage. Read Matthew 3:7–10 and Mark 6:14–20 to see how the New Testament "Elijah," John the Baptist, took off on the same confrontational track. Compare the willingness of these two men to deliver a "politically incorrect" message in the presence of entrenched governmental evil. What principles can we learn from their example?

2. Compare what you've learned about Obadiah to the story of Nicodemus in John 3:1–21. What do these men have in common? What do they have in common with many Christian men in today's world?

3. Right in the middle of a fast-paced account of Elijah, Ahab, Jezebel, and Obadiah, the biblical writer tells a story about a widow and her son in a place called Zarephath (1 Kings 17:7–24). The placement of this story seems strange. Why do you think the Holy Spirit might have directed the writer to place this little "aside" right in the middle of the larger story? What lessons can we learn from this brief but amazing encounter?

4. Read again Warren Wiersbe's contrast of two godly but very different men:

   > Elijah was serving the Lord publicly and without fear; Obadiah was serving Ahab and trying to serve the Lord secretly. Elijah was "outside the camp" (Hebrews 13:13); Obadiah was inside the court. Elijah knew the will of God; Obadiah did not know what was going on. While Elijah was laboring to save the nation, Obadiah was out looking for grass to save the horse and mules. When Elijah confronted Obadiah, the frightened servant did not trust the prophet. And note that Obadiah had to "brag" about his secret service to impress Elijah with his devotion.

   As we view the emerging cultural war exploding on all sides of us, what does an "Elijah" look like in today's America? What does an "Obadiah" look like?

9

FIGHTING THE GOOD FIGHT

If the foundations are destroyed,
what can the righteous do?
PSALM 11:3

I had a pretty good idea why they wanted to meet.

While speaking at a men's conference, I met a group of guys who were all in the same accountability group. They asked if we might be able to get together for a half hour or so. We decided to meet that night after the evening session.

I knew from our initial conversation that although these six guys were in a group that met every week, they were from two different churches. It was when they told me which two churches they were members of that I had a pretty strong clue as to what they wanted to discuss. It really didn't take a genius to figure it out.

What they had in common was this. Both groups of men had senior pastors who had been asked to step down because of moral failure in their personal lives. And it had devastated both churches.

These two churches were not small. As a result, the failure of both pastors sent Richter-scale shock waves up and down their part of the country. Both of these pastors had very high profiles. Both were remarkably gifted speakers. They could mesmerize people with their humor, their exposition, and their personalities. As a result, their churches were growing with unbelievable strides. Thousands of people were coming to hear each of these men.

That's why their fall was so cataclysmic. They affected thousands as they climbed the ladder of success, and they affected even more when they fell off.

What was interesting was that I met both of these men fifteen years ago. I spent some time with each of them. After spending the afternoon with the first pastor, I remember being somewhat stunned as I drove home. As Mary and I talked over dinner, I told her a little bit of our conversation. To tell you the truth, it was eye opening to spend several hours with this guy. Although we had just met, a mutual friend was with us, with whom he felt very comfortable. As a result his guard was down. That's why at dinner that night I said something that really surprised my wife.

"Mary, I think that guy is headed for a major fall."

I'm no prophet. But something was obviously wrong in this man's life, and the unguarded signals were so clear that even I could see them.

He talked freely of his dreams, his aspirations, the books he was reading, and his latest successes. What was very clear was that there were a number of influences in his life, but the New Testament apparently wasn't one of them. He sounded like a guy looking to get to the top and get there in a hurry.

That's what he did. He got to the top in a hurry. He got there so fast that he fell off. It happened ten years after our meeting. After allegations of sexual involvement with a woman associate, he divorced his wife and left his children.

I had met the other pastor about a year later, and we had the opportunity to spend an entire weekend together. What a great weekend that was. This guy had a love for Jesus Christ and a love for the Scriptures that was very apparent. He also seemed to have a great love for his wife. He talked about her throughout the weekend and how they were so very careful to protect their marriage and sustain it. This guy was solid. He was the exact opposite of the other pastor. I greatly benefited from our time together and wished that it could have continued. That's why I was absolutely shocked to hear that he had resigned from his church because of moral reasons. I was stunned, jarred, startled, and shaken. I was also in a state of disbelief. In fact, I didn't believe it until I talked with his associate and the facts were confirmed.

FIGHTIN' FOR THE BRAND

The Christian life is a violent life. Does that surprise you? It shouldn't. The Christian life is a life of warfare, a life of high-stakes spiritual combat. The Bible clearly states that we are in a battle with the world, the flesh, and the devil. That's precisely why Paul told Timothy to "fight the good fight."

Satan may be many things, but he is no fool. He is very strategic in his efforts. That's why he goes after those in leadership. If a highly visible spiritual leader can be brought down, then the fallout will be great. That's why we should be praying for our pastors and for other leaders who have been given a place in ministry.

It's also why we should be praying for ourselves.

You don't have to be a well-known speaker to be the recipient of the enemy's attack. He is more than happy to bring down a Sunday school teacher or any other person of influence in a local congregation. That's why we all have to stand tall and fight the good fight.

The question that these brokenhearted church leaders put before me that evening was this: "How is it that men who have had such influence in the body of Christ can suddenly fall into sexual immorality?"

The answer I offered was that it probably wasn't sudden. It seemed sudden, but that's only because we couldn't see the private choices that these men had been making over the last few years. When sexual immorality hits in the life of a spiritual leader, it is usually the accumulated, tragic result of a series of poor and very private choices.

That's what Paul was trying to get across to Timothy. Paul wanted Timothy to be successful. That's why Paul's words to this young pastor have such relevance to all of us who want to be people of character. In fact, it is impossible to climb the character ladder without applying these words to our lives. Every day.

This command I entrust to you, Timothy, my son, in accordance with
the prophecies previously made concerning you, that by them you
may fight the good fight. (1 Timothy 1:18)

THE MENTORING EPISTLES

The New Testament letters of 1 and 2 Timothy, along with Titus, are frequently
called the Pastoral Epistles. Timothy and Titus were young pastors, and Paul
was writing to them to give some tangible principles that would enable them
to be successful in their work. Today, we might say that Paul was mentoring
these young men.

What is a mentor? John Gardner says that a mentor is an older person
who actively helps young people along the road to leadership—as a friend, an
advisor, a teacher, a coach, a listener, or a resource. Gardner writes that "mentoring may be as formal as a master-apprentice relationship or as informal as
an older friend helping a younger one."[99]

If you ever benefited from the wisdom and counsel of an older person
who took an interest in you, then you know firsthand how meaningful a mentor can be to a younger person. And it's people who have personally profited
from that kind of valued relationship who make excellent mentors themselves.

Paul and Timothy had a father-son relationship. They were exceptionally
close and Paul had a vested interest in Timothy's well-being. Timothy was a
young man in a difficult situation (it's funny how often that is the case!).

Timothy was not happy. He was in over his head at Ephesus. But Paul
needed Timothy to do at least three things: appoint elders in the church, combat false doctrine and false teachers, and supervise the church as Paul's personal representative. That was a tall order for a young man like Timothy.

Timothy's main problem was that he wasn't Paul. He didn't have Paul's age
or wisdom or in-your-face personality. Timothy was a nonconfronter in a situation that cried out for confrontation.

NO PLACE TO RUN

The real estate broker was driving slowly down a residential street looking for
a new listing. As he came to the house, he noticed a little boy next door strain-

ing to reach the doorbell. The little boy was up as far as he could get on his tiptoes, but he still couldn't reach the doorbell.

The man smiled as he watched the scene and then walked over to the door and rang the doorbell for the little fellow. The little boy looked up at the man and said, "Now *run!*"

Paul's young buddy Timothy wanted to run, too.

That's why earlier in the chapter, in verse 2, Paul had to urge him to "remain on at Ephesus." Timothy didn't want to stick around Ephesus. He wanted to find the back door and slip through it as soon as possible. But Paul had other plans for him. Paul wanted him to "fight the good fight." In other words, it was time for Timothy to stand tall.

Mentors know when their protégés need some encouragement. That's why Paul reminded Timothy of the prophecies that were made concerning him. We are not privy to the content of these prophecies, but apparently someone, speaking by the Spirit, predicted the kind of ministry Timothy would have. These prophecies were a source of encouragement to the young pastor. That's why Paul brought them up.

Paul was Timothy's coach. It's almost as though Paul, although writing from a distance, was trying to psych Timothy up for the game, not unlike a coach in a locker room. Paul wanted Timothy to get in there and fight!

But Timothy hated fighting. It just wasn't his personality.

I remember very well the first root canal I ever had. I was twelve years old, and my tooth started to abscess one night as we were eating dinner. My mom called the dentist, and he said to bring me right in. As I was stepping into the room for my root canal, Cassius Clay was stepping into the ring to meet Sonny Liston. It was Tuesday evening, February 25, 1964, 8:45 P.M. in Miami for the boxing match, and 5:45 P.M. in San Francisco for the root canal. My dentist had the fight going full blast on the radio as he was working on me.

This was the first big fight of Cassius Clay's career. We now know Cassius Clay as Muhammad Ali, one of the greatest fighters of all time. But on that night, he was just a young, loudmouthed kid, up against the man known as the "The Bear." I can remember the week before the fight seeing a full-page picture of Sonny Liston and thinking to myself, *That guy is the meanest and toughest guy I've ever seen. Cassius Clay is going to get killed.*

That was pretty much the consensus before the fight. Hardly anyone gave

Clay a chance. I didn't think I'd survive the root canal or that Clay would survive Liston. But I was wrong on both counts. My dentist knocked out the knotty nerve and Clay knocked out the menacing bear.

Timothy was no Cassius Clay. It wasn't his personality. Yet he was called to "fight the good fight." And so are we. We are called to fight it every day. But here's the question—and it is an extremely important question.

How do I fight the good fight?

The reason that question is so critical is that so many in the body of Christ are not fighting the good fight. They have been disqualified, and they have not gone the distance.

I want to fight the good fight. Timothy wanted to fight the good fight. The question is *how*. How do I do it?

Paul gives the answer in the next verse. "Keeping faith and a good conscience, which some have rejected and suffered shipwreck in regard to their faith" (1 Timothy 1:19).

Keeping Faith and a Good Conscience

Yogi Berra once said, "If you come to a fork in the road, take it." Now, that doesn't make much sense. Usually a fork means you have to go left or go right. How does one fight the good fight? By doing two things: keeping faith and a good conscience. You have to do both. If you just keep faith, then you won't fight the good fight. If you just keep a good conscience, you won't fight the good fight. You have to do both. Let's take them in order.

"Keeping faith."

What in the world does that mean? Well, let's think it through. Where does faith come from? Ephesians 2:8 is very clear that faith is a gift of God. But how does God distribute this faith? Through what means does faith come into our lives? According to Romans 10:17: "Faith comes from hearing, and hearing by the word of Christ."

It is impossible to separate faith from the Word of God. And what is the Word of God? According to Hebrews 4:12, the "word of God is living and active and sharper than any two-edged sword, and piercing as far as the division of soul and spirit, of both joints and marrow, and able to judge the thoughts and intentions of the heart."

When Paul instructs Timothy to fight the good fight by "keeping faith," Paul is referring to the doctrinal purity that comes only from the Word of God. He is reminding Timothy that he must stay in the Word of God if his faith is going to remain clear, clean, and pure.

The enemy loves to downplay the importance of the Bible in our lives. That's why he works so hard to keep us from interacting with Scripture! Mark this: If I'm not in the Word, it is *impossible* for me to fight the good fight. Moses certainly didn't downplay Scripture. Note his words in Deuteronomy 32:46–47: "Take to your heart all the words which I am warning you today, which you shall command your sons to observe carefully, even all the words of this law. For it is not an idle word for you; indeed *it is your life*" (emphasis mine).

That's a pretty strong statement. But it fits perfectly with what Jesus said about the character of Scripture. When Jesus was being tempted by Satan in the wilderness, He responded to the first temptation with the words, "It is written, Man shall not live by bread alone, but on every word that proceeds out of the mouth of God." We live off of the Scripture. It is our life. The word of God contains the spiritual vitamins and minerals that we need to "fight the good fight." Without the nutrition of the Scripture, it is impossible to fight well. Without the Scripture there is no vitality, no energy, no health. No wonder Oswald Chambers said:

> The mere reading of the Word of God has power to communicate the life of God to us mentally, morally, and spiritually. God makes the words of the Bible a sacrament, i.e., the means whereby we partake of His life, it is one of His secret doors for the communication of His life to us.[100]

No wonder the enemy wants to keep me away from my Bible!

"*A good conscience.*"

But there's a second aspect to fighting the good faith. Paul emphasized to Timothy that he must keep a "*good conscience.*" That's the tough part about fighting the good fight. This war is fought on two fronts. We find ourselves fighting on both fronts simultaneously. If you put all of your effort into keeping faith, you will be leaving your flank wide open. Or if you are completely focused on keeping a good conscience, you are just as vulnerable. In order to fight the good fight, we have to do both. We have to be keeping faith *and* a good conscience. At the same time.

The priority of a good conscience is a theme Paul rides hard all the way through this letter to Timothy. That makes complete sense, since 1 Timothy is really a handbook on spiritual leadership. It's impossible to be an effective spiritual leader without paying attention to the condition of one's conscience.

A couple of years ago I was invited to speak to a chapel service for the Cincinnati Bengals. I had my two boys with me, and we had a great time meeting many of the players at chapel and then watching the Bengals play the Steelers on a crisp December afternoon in fifteen-degree weather. We went through a lot of hot chocolate that afternoon! We had some free time after the chapel service and before the kickoff, so I was reading the Sunday sports page.

That's when my eye caught the NFL injury list for that weekend's games around the league. The injury list contains the name of each injured player and the particular injury they are experiencing (knee, Achilles tendon, wrist, etc.). Each player is then listed as out, probable, or doubtful.

On that particular list were the names of around fifty players. These men had an incredible list of injuries: broken arms, broken legs, broken jaws, pulled hamstrings, turf toes, and hyperextended elbows. But what was fascinating to me was that none of those players was on the injury list for leprosy. That's right. Leprosy.

Most of us in this country don't think about leprosy. We may think of the possibilities of having a heart attack, or some type of cancer, but unless I miss my guess, the idea that you might get leprosy has never crossed your mind. Generally speaking, leprosy is not an American disease, although there is a leprosarium still functioning in Louisiana. But leprosy is associated more with Third World countries than with the United States. Consequently, most of us have very little understanding of what leprosy really is.

As a young boy, I remember watching a movie that a missionary from India was showing to our church. It was my first exposure to leprosy. I'll never forget seeing those black and white images of people who had lost their toes, feet, fingers, and hands. I thought for some reason leprosy was a disease of the skin. Years later I found out leprosy is not a skin disease, it's a *nerve* disease.

A person with leprosy has lost the ability to feel. In a Third World country, a leprous man can be walking down a street barefoot, step on a piece of glass, and keep right on walking. He doesn't even realize there's an injury, because there is no pain. No feeling. Nothing. It's not until he looks down and sees the blood that he realizes something is wrong. By that time, the hunk of glass may have worked its way further up into his foot. A normal person would feel all of these things, but the person with leprosy is unable to feel the throbbing sensations.

A woman with leprosy could pick up a cast iron skillet and not even realize the skillet was horribly hot, even as it seared the skin right off of her hand. That's the problem with leprosy. Lepers have lost the ability to feel because their nerves are dead. That's how they wind up losing toes, feet, fingers, and hands.

There is a spiritual nerve located deep down in every one of us. It is the nerve of conscience. You have heard it said, "Let conscience be your guide." That's not quite right. The guide to right and wrong is the Scripture. The Bible is the basis of our moral value system. Conscience is a nerve that begins to pulsate when we depart from what we know to be right. As we move from right toward wrong, the nerve of conscience begins to send messages to us. It lets us know something is wrong. It warns us that we are moving into dangerous territory.

There is a tragic explanation in 1 Timothy of something that is going to happen in the last days. In 1 Timothy 4:1, Paul tells Timothy: "The Spirit explicitly says that in later times some will fall away from the faith, paying attention to deceitful spirits and doctrines of demons."

What is interesting here is the reason some will fall away. They have not kept faith! Instead of listening to the doctrinal purity of the Word of God, they have paid attention to deceitful spirits and doctrines of demons! But Paul continues in the next verse to explain how they paid attention to such wrong doctrine. They listened to false teachers. Note Paul's explanation of *why* certain men will be false teachers: "By means of the hypocrisy of liars *seared in their own conscience* as with a branding iron" (1 Timothy 4:2, emphasis mine).

Did you catch the significance of what Paul said? The reason these men can teach such doctrinal deceit, which they *know* to be wrong, is because they are men without conscience. It's almost as though they took a white-hot poker and thrust it down deep into the depths of their souls. These men have cauterized their own consciences, and they don't feel anything anymore. They are spiritual lepers.

How does one become a spiritual leper? Believe me, there are many of them walking around. One becomes a spiritual leper by consistently *not* keeping a good conscience. A spiritual leper is someone who consistently chooses not to listen to his conscience when his conscience indicates that he is deviating from what he knows to be true. It's not that these folks don't know what is right. The issue is that they refuse to *do* what is right.

Every time the Spirit of God impresses our conscience and we fail to respond to His prompting, we are coating our sensitive nerve with another layer of resistance, and we are taking a step toward leprosy. Over a long period of time, our consciences become hard and callus.

That is a very dangerous state for any nerve. Especially the nerve of conscience. It is possible for that nerve to become so callus that when the Holy Spirit touches, it feels absolutely nothing. Not even one impulse.

That, my friends, is a graphic description of a spiritual leper. And they are everywhere.

The key to keeping a good conscience is not so much in the big choices, but the little ones. It's those seemingly tiny choices of the inner man that no one else ever sees. That's why we are so shocked when we hear about the immorality of a very public preacher. Perhaps we have benefited greatly from the person's teachings over the radio or through cassette tapes. The problem is this: You can't look into someone's conscience over the radio. You can't look into a conscience at all. But that's where the real fight takes place. Only the Holy Spirit, the enemy, and we, are able to see into that very private arena.

Standing tall in private is just as important as standing tall in public. Maybe more so.

Have you noticed that wherever there is sexual immorality, there is also deceit? Deceit and sexual immorality always go hand in hand. Because when something is wrong in our lives—such as sexual immorality—we will go to great lengths in order to deceive others about the reality of the situation. But before we deceive others, we first deceive ourselves. Before we lie to others, we first lie to ourselves. And that's where heeding the first impulses of the Holy Spirit on our nerves of conscience can save us from choices that will cause our lives to completely unravel. Lying must be nipped in the bud. It is lying out of control that leads to deceit of ourselves, our spouses, our children, and our friends.

Let me give you a personal example.

THE PRICE OF A CLEAN CONSCIENCE

A number of years ago, when Mary and I were pulling out of our tough chapter, we were really counting our pennies. We were even counting our halfpennies. In order to make our budget stretch even further, we decided that I would take my lunch to the office rather than buy lunch. I committed to do that every day. No problem.

But one particular morning was extremely hectic. The alarm didn't go off, and everyone was late. As I hustled to get out the door, I forgot my lunch. But I didn't realize it until later. I was studying that morning for my sermon on Sunday. As lunchtime approached, I went to get my lunch and then realized I had left it at home. I decided just to keep studying through my normal lunchtime because I really could use the extra time.

By about two-thirty, however, I started to get a headache, and I usually don't get headaches. I then realized I hadn't eaten since about seven o'clock that morning.

I made a quick run over to McDonald's and ordered a Quarter Pounder with cheese and a medium Diet Coke. (I'm sort of a health nut.) By the time I actually ate it was three o'clock in the afternoon. I went back to the office, did some more studying, and left for home a little earlier than usual. We were going to some event that evening as a family, and it required about an hour's drive in rush-hour traffic. We had planned to have an early dinner so we could get a head start on traffic and hopefully arrive at our destination on time.

As I walked in the door, the kids were already at the table. "Your timing is perfect," Mary said. "We're ready to eat!"

As I sat down, she added, "You forgot your lunch today. What did you do for lunch?"

I replied, "I didn't eat lunch."

That's what is known as a lie.

Mary said, "You must really be hungry if you didn't eat lunch."

"I sure am!"

I wasn't. I had just eaten about an hour and a half before at McDonald's. I sat down and ate enough to make it look like I was indeed hungry when in actuality I wasn't hungry at all.

Several days later I was in my office, going over my sermon notes for Sunday. I was done with my preparation and was going over my outline and praying that God would be pleased to use me that coming Sunday. I was asking Him to speak through me in a powerful way to communicate the message of His Word. It was a time of quiet meditation. No one else was in the room. Just me, my Bible, and my notes.

And the Holy Spirit.

As I was praying, I suddenly felt something. What I felt was one of my nerves. To be more specific, it was the nerve of conscience. Something was flicking the nerve of my conscience. I knew who was doing it, and I knew what it was about. It was the Holy Spirit. He was impressing my conscience that I had deviated from what I knew to be right and true. I had lied to my wife. That's when the rationalizations started.

It was only $2.89. What's $2.89? It's no big deal.

Another flick.

So I didn't tell her the truth. I just won't do it again.

Another flick. A little stronger this time.

If I tell her that I lied to her, she's going to think I'm a real jerk. My credibility isn't worth destroying over $2.89.

It was right there that I was on dangerous territory. My credibility was already gone. Mary just didn't know about it. Finally, I did what I really wanted to avoid. I picked up the phone and dialed. Mary answered.

"Mary? How's it going?"

"Fine, sweetheart. What's up?"

"Mary, um, do you remember the other day when I forgot my lunch and when I got home you asked me what I did for lunch and I said that I didn't eat lunch?"

"Sure I do."

"Well, I ate lunch. I went to McDonald's and spent $2.89 for a Quarter Pounder with cheese and a medium Diet Coke."

"Steve," she said with amusement, "why didn't you just tell me?"

"I honestly don't know," I replied. "Maybe I was embarrassed that I broke my promise about eating lunch out. But whatever the reason, I'm calling to tell you that I lied to you. Mary, would you forgive me for lying to you?"

"Of course I forgive you. Thanks for calling and telling me the truth."

I'll be honest with you. I really didn't want to make that call. After all, it was only $2.89. But in reality, a lot more was at stake than $2.89.

What was at stake was the trust in my marriage.

What was at stake was letting a small crack run unchecked in the sanctity of our home.

What was at stake was whether or not I was going to fight the good fight or just pretend to fight sin in my own life.

So I made the call. Too much was on the line to let it pass.

How does a man in spiritual leadership who has had such an impact in your life suddenly fall into sexual immorality? Well, it starts with something around $2.89. Something small. Something insignificant. Instead of obeying the nudge of the Holy Spirit, he lets it pass. Then when the next small thing happens, well, he lets that one go, too. And over a period of weeks and months, a series of seemingly small and insignificant choices are being made that no one else sees. The Spirit of God is trying to get the man's attention, but he is now walking around with a nerve that has become more callus. And the more callus the nerve, the easier it is to ignore the Spirit of God.

Then one day, "she" walks into his life. He will soon be in a situation that would have been absolutely unthinkable just a year or two ago. But now it's not only possible, it's also probable. Why? Because that nerve of conscience, which helps us fight the good fight, has been severely damaged by neglect. Long before a spiritual leader ever climbs into the bed of immorality, God has been trying to get his attention.

But there is nerve damage. Severe nerve damage.

At that first "private" meeting, just to have lunch or to meet to talk about some church activity, you can be sure the Spirit of God twinged that minister's conscience and at that moment he knew the meeting was inappropriate. But instead of heeding the impulse of the Spirit on his nerve of conscience, they decided to meet again. Once again, the Holy Spirit hit the nerve. But he didn't respond. On and on it goes. That is the pattern that leads to sexual immorality in the life of anyone. And believe it or not, it can start with something as small as $2.89.

What's the $2.89 in your life? Have you dealt with it? Or are you still rationalizing and coddling it?

That's why it is so important to heed the Spirit's prompting early. If we hesitate, if we rationalize, if we try to bypass the twinging nerve of conscience, we are only going to find ourselves in an increasingly tangled web of emotions that get more and more difficult to break away from.

How do we avoid becoming trapped in Satan's deceptive web? It's simple. We determine to acknowledge the Holy Spirit every time He touches our inner nerve of conscience. That's how He gets our attention. What happens if we don't quickly acknowledge the Spirit's promptings? Then we are on our way to shipwreck. At least that's the metaphor Paul uses to describe it.

THREE SHIPS THAT NEVER SAILED HOME

What do the *Titanic*, the *Hymenaeus*, and the *Alexander* have in common? All three experienced horrible shipwrecks.

But only the *Titanic* was a ship. Hymenaeus and Alexander were men.

The *Titanic* has been found at the bottom of the Atlantic. Hymenaeus and Alexander can be found on the pages of the New Testament. Specifically in 1 Timothy:

> Keeping faith and a good conscience, which some have rejected and suffered shipwreck in regard to their faith. Among these are Hymenaeus and Alexander, whom I have delivered over to Satan, so that they may be taught not to blaspheme. (1:19–20)

Shipwrecked lives, shipwrecked dreams, shipwrecked families, and shipwrecked churches. Shipwrecks are always great tragedies. But to shipwreck spiritually is the greatest tragedy of all. That's what happened to Hymenaeus and Alexander. And it's happening with increasing frequency in the church today.

We are missing a great deal of the puzzle that makes up the story of Hymenaeus and Alexander. But Paul knew the missing pieces and so did Timothy. That's why he mentioned them to Timothy. What we do know is that they shipwrecked. And they shipwrecked for one of two reasons:

- They didn't keep sound doctrine.
- They didn't keep a good conscience.

The Exxon *Valdez* shipwrecked and coated the Alaska coastline with oil. As I wrote these words, the 89,700-ton tanker *Braer* had run aground in the Shetland Islands of Scotland. Shipwrecks happen all the time.

Yet there is more than one way to be shipwrecked. And in the body of Christ, the amount of shipwrecks that are attributed to sexual immorality are growing every day. Paul wanted Timothy to fight the good fight. That's why he put such an emphasis on keeping faith and a good conscience. Both must be well in hand if our credibility is to be restored. Our walk must back up our talk.

The same question burned in the minds of the six men I met with at the men's conference: "How in the world did our pastor get involved in immorality?" I asked them if they were in the morning session, and they nodded that they were. In that session I taught the concepts and the passage that is in this chapter. As we thought through the circumstances of each pastor, the answer started to emerge.

The first pastor shipwrecked because he had not kept faith. He became enamored with popular psychology. His love for the Scripture gradually gave way to desire to speak "relevant" messages in the pulpit. He gradually lost his ability to see how relevant the Scriptures really are. Truth is always relevant. He shipwrecked because he lost his love for the purity of the Word, and as he lost his commitment to the Scripture, his conscience started to give way as well.

The second pastor was on the other end of the spectrum. He loved the Scriptures and was powerful in the Scriptures. But he allowed himself to get into some compromising situations. When a close friend approached him about it, he explained the situation away as harmless. I'm sure that Another approached him as well over the years—the Holy Spirit. But he didn't respond to those impulses on the nerve of his conscience, and that's how he shipwrecked. He was doctrinally pure, but he still shipwrecked.

Both of these men were gifted. That's why some are attempting to get them back into "ministry," even when there has been repentance that is shallow at best. "They are so gifted!" comes the reply. There can be no denying their giftedness. But the issue is not giftedness; it is character.

John Luther states the matter brilliantly.

Good character is more to be praised than outstanding talent. Most talents are, to some extent, a gift. Good character, by contrast, is not given to us. We have to build it piece by piece, thought by thought, choice by choice, which requires great courage and determination.[101]

It's easy to point at spiritual leaders and see their weaknesses. But the question that I pose to you is the one that I frequently pose to myself: Are you fighting the good fight? Are you standing tall in private, when no one sees? Are you keeping faith and a good conscience? Those are questions that only you can answer.

There is an old poem that sums up Paul's instruction to young Timothy:

When wealth is lost, nothing is lost;
When health is lost, something is lost;
When character is lost, everything is lost.

Let me be very direct. If you are involved in some type of sexual sin, please don't take a stand against homosexuality in your community. Please don't attend a school board meeting and voice your conviction against a sex education curriculum. And please...don't join a church board or teach a Sunday school class. Why? Because you can be sure your sin will find you out. When it does, the moral stands that you took will be discredited.

And so will the name of Jesus Christ.

If there is any kind of sin in your life that you have not confessed, then it is impossible for you to fight the good fight. You may fight, but it won't be the good fight.

And that's no fight at all.

WALKING TALL

1. I have stated that the Christian life is a violent life. In what way is this more—or less—apparent in our day than it was in our fathers' and grandfathers' generations? Review Peter's strong counsel to men in 1 Peter 5:1–11. What are three or four key principles the apostle offers for fighting the good—and sometimes violent—fight?

2. Young Timothy was incredibly blessed to have a loyal, battle-scarred veteran in his corner. When Paul commanded Timothy to "fight the good fight," Timothy knew he had a lot more than his friend's verbal backing. He had Paul's example, Paul's abiding interest and concern, and Paul's constant prayers behind him. Discuss the role of mentors among Christian men in the church. When have you benefited most from a concerned older man willing to stay in your corner? When have you longed for such an individual, but never found one? How can guys today who want to fight the good fight find a mentor...or become one?

3. What are some of the ways we men can encourage each other to "keep faith" by staying in the Word?

4. Reflect on a time when you attempted to "stuff" the voice of your conscience in an area of your life. Were you "successful" in your attempts? What happened as a result? How can we restore the nerve of conscience after it has been deadened by repeated disobedience? How can we help each other as men to restore and maintain a good conscience?

5. Review Proverbs 20:30; 27:5–6; 28:23 and Psalm 141:4–5. What would you do if you suspected that one of your close Christian friends was headed toward moral shipwreck? What would the risks be of damaging your relationship—or getting punched in the mouth? What would the risks be of remaining quiet and turning a blind eye?

10

SEVEN WAYS TO HELP YOUR KIDS STAND TALL

Without God, we cannot. Without us, God will not.
AUGUSTINE

The prayer of a righteous man is powerful and effective.
JAMES

E li Whitney is famous for inventing the cotton gin. But Whitney didn't get his money from the cotton gin. Whitney became a wealthy man by inventing and manufacturing firearms. One of the men he teamed up with was Sam Colt.

Colt was a marketing genius who knew how to use advertising to spread the fame of the Colt revolvers. But Whitney was the actual hands-on genius. It was the collective efforts of Sam Colt and Eli Whitney that formulated one of the most popular weapons in the Old West that eventually brought law and order to a rapidly changing society.

Another powerful weapon in the Old West was the printing press. But it was bigger than just the Old West. The printing press changed the whole world. And it was Johannes Gutenberg, a man who lived back in the 1400s, who came up with it. How in the world did Gutenberg come up with an invention that changed the world? He did it by connecting two things that were previously unconnected.

Gutenberg took the wine press and the coin punch and came up with the printing press. The function of the wine press was to apply a force over a large area in order to squeeze juice out of grapes. The purpose of the coin punch was to leave an image on a small area such as a gold coin.[102] Johannes took two very good concepts and turned them into something revolutionary.

When you look at your kids, what do you see? Do you see them as they are now...or do you see them as what they will become? I think a lot of guys look at their four-year-olds and just see four-year-olds. And we need to value them and appreciate them as four-year-olds. But on the other hand, we also need to clearly see that these four-year-olds won't always be four. In ten years, they'll be fourteen, chompin' at the bit to get their driver's licenses in a couple of years.

They will also be under tremendous peer pressure.

In just ten years, your four-year-old will be making some of the most critical choices of his entire life. The decision he will make every day is whether he will be a leader or a follower.

I'm convinced that we need to "Gutenberg" our kids. Just as Johannes took a press and a punch and turned them into a printing press, so we dads need to take our kids and shape their character, so we turn them into leaders. Now obviously some kids are natural leaders. They'll grab the initiative and make things happen. But what I'm talking about is turning your kids into *moral* and *spiritual* leaders. I'm talking about turning your kids into men and women of character who can make the kind of tough character choices that few leaders in our contemporary world seem able to make.

The time to begin doing that is now.

Something happens when a kid hits adolescence. When kids are small, they tend to think their dad hung the moon. When kids hit adolescence, sometimes they begin to think their dad should go to the moon. To take it a step further, when a boy or girl hits adolescence, one of two things is going to happen. An adolescent will either go to his peers and critique his parents, or go to his parents and critique his peers. Obviously, we want our kids to come to us.

To put it another way, a child is going to be either a leader or a follower. Teenagers are deciding this every day of their lives. There is pressure to do drugs, have sex, and do whatever it is that everyone else is doing. So how do we combat that? We combat it by Gutenberging our kids into leaders. And we get after it right away.

Roger von Oech tells the story of a terrible plague that swept through Lithuania. No one could quite figure it out.

What was curious about this disease was its grip on its victim; as soon as the person contracted it, he would go into a very deep almost death-like coma. Most individuals would die within twenty-four hours, but occasionally a hardy soul would make it back to the full bloom of health. The problem was that since early eighteenth-century medical technology wasn't very advanced, the unafflicted had quite a difficult time telling whether a victim was dead or alive. This didn't matter too much, though, because most of the people were, in fact, dead.

Then one day it was discovered that someone had been buried alive. This alarmed the townspeople, so they called a town meeting to decide what should be done to prevent such a situation from happening again. After much discussion, most people agreed on the following solution. They decided to put food and water in every casket next to the body. They would even put an air hole up from the casket to the earth's surface. These procedures would be expensive, but they would be more than worthwhile if they would save some people's lives.

Another group came up with a second, less expensive, right answer. They proposed implanting a twelve inch long stake in every coffin lid directly over where the victim's heart would be. Then whatever doubts there were about whether the person was dead or alive would be eliminated as soon as the coffin lid was closed. [103]

Thousands of adolescents are buried alive by peer pressure each year. Not only are they buried alive, but in each coffin there's a twelve-inch stake that goes right into their hearts. A number of twelve-, thirteen-, and fourteen-year-old kids (not to mention fifteen-, sixteen-, and seventeen-) are emotionally killed because they haven't been *trained* to withstand the pressure from their peers. Good dads make sure their kids have airholes and plenty of emotional food and water. They also plan way in advance to keep the coffin of a sick and godless culture from slamming shut on their adolescent.

In our MTV culture, the majority of teenagers are swimming with the current (and so are their parents). I want my kids to swim upstream. I don't want my kids to be swept along in the current of peer pressure. I want them to be secure enough in who they are and what they believe that they will be confident to swim *against* the current. Followers go with the current. Leaders go against it.

Leadership: What Is It?

What is leadership? That's a question that has received a lot of attention. A friend of mine wrote his doctoral dissertation on leadership and found 165 published definitions. Some of those definitions are pretty complex and dazzling. Dr. Howard Hendricks, distinguished professor at Dallas Theological Seminary, has come up with the best definition of a leader I've ever heard. According to Dr. Hendricks, "A leader is someone who leads." Don't let the simplicity of that definition fool you. It is pregnant with meaning.

Recently a man handed me his business card. It was impressive. Nicely designed. Gold-embossed logo. It listed his position as chief executive officer and president. I later found out this man is a poor excuse for a leader. Yet his card is impressive. This man has positional leadership, but an illustrious business card or title doesn't make someone a leader. As John Gardner puts it:

> We must not confuse leadership with status. Even in large corporations and government agencies, the top-ranking person may simply be bureaucrat number 1. We have all occasionally encountered the top persons who couldn't lead a squad of seven-year-olds to the ice cream counter.[104]

In other words, you are only a leader if you lead.

Leaders come in many forms, with many styles and diverse qualities. There are quiet leaders and leaders one can hear in the next county.

Some find their strength in eloquence, some in judgment, some in courage....

The fact that there are many kinds of leaders has implications for leadership education. Most of those seeking to develop young potential leaders have in mind one ideal model that is inevitably constricting. We should give young people a sense of the many kinds of leaders and styles of leadership, and encourage them to move toward those models that are right for them.[105]

It's important we distinguish between leading and "managing." Managing is usually tied in with some type of organizational structure. The true leader may have no organizational structure at all. He simply leads.

In 1947, a professor at the University of Chicago, Dr. Chandrasekhar, was scheduled to teach a class in advanced astrophysics. The professor was living in Wisconsin, where he was doing some research for an upcoming conference. His plan was to commute to Chicago twice a week, even though the class was held during the winter quarter and he would encounter the very worst weather the Midwest could throw at him.

The professor had second thoughts about teaching the class when he heard that only two students had signed up for his course. He thought of the distance; he thought of the time away from his family; and he thought of the snow and ice. But then he thought of the two students. He decided to follow through on his commitment to teach. He had obviously hoped for more than two students, yet perhaps those two students would be worth the time investment.

Ten years later, Dr. Chandrasekhar was very pleased to hear that the two young men who made up his class were progressing along quite nicely. Chen Ning Yang and Tsung-Dao Lee were both awarded the Nobel Prize in physics in 1957. In 1983, Dr. Chandrasekhar was awarded the same honor. You might say the class was worth the effort. The professor who demonstrated his leadership in being willing to teach just two young, motivated students obviously passed along some values and character as well as a syllabus.

Gentlemen, your kids are your students. You're teaching a class on leadership every day. And whether you realize it or not, they are watching your example like hawks. You may have only one or two students, but a man with vision knows that the opportunity to shape the lives of his children with godly character is simply too good to pass up. It's worth whatever sacrifice is necessary.

I've been thinking about this process of turning kids into leaders for quite some time. Not only have I been thinking about it, but I have also been *working* on it. I have some good friends who are in the same process. From time to time we will compare notes for the simple reason that none of us really has our act together. So we check in with one another as much as possible and talk shop about raising our kids to be leaders.

I have come up with seven principles that could help your kids stand tall. Interestingly enough, I see all seven in the leadership style of our old friend Mordecai. Mordecai did a pretty fair job of raising Esther to be a leader. His leadership of Esther gave her what it took to be a leader when her life was literally on the line.

1. Be a leader yourself.

Dave Johnson is a friend of mine in San Jose who rides for the brand. For years Dave rode for the brand on a Harley. But now he rides in a patrol car. Dave is a police officer in San Jose who wrote a fascinating book about his experiences as a street cop. Dave has plenty of stories that are hilarious, but here's one that could make you weep:

> Frank and I had just finished a call and climbed into our police cars.... As I started my car, I heard the police radio call out Frank's unit number. The dispatcher reported a young boy missing from his residence. I heard the address and the description: two years old, wearing tennis shoes, coveralls, and a light blue T-shirt. The dispatcher said the mother had lain down on the couch and fallen asleep, and discovered the boy missing when she awoke fifteen minutes later.
>
> Frank acknowledged the call and began driving to the address. I picked up my radio and told the dispatcher I would respond to the area to help in the search.
>
> I was driving directly behind Frank's car. Our sergeant, Dennis Busch, had also heard the call and, because he was nearby, radioed back that he would also respond.
>
> Suddenly the dispatcher alerted Frank, Dennis, and myself: "The

lost boy has been located—in the next-door neighbor's swimming pool."

Adrenaline shot through my veins as I reached for the control switch to activate my red lights. I saw Frank's lights jump on at the same time. We both accelerated. I began praying that the people who found the boy knew CPR—cardio-pulmonary resuscitation—and were attempting to revive him.

As Frank and I rounded the corner near the address, we saw several men standing on the sidewalk in front of a house. Dennis was just getting out of his police car and talking with the group of people. As I began getting out of my car, I suddenly saw Dennis bolt toward a gate at the side of the house. As Frank and I got closer, one of the men pointed and told us what he must have told Dennis: "The boy's in the pool in that backyard." I could hardly believe what I'd heard.

Frank and I both ran through a narrow side yard that led to the swimming pool. As we rounded the corner of the house we could see Dennis pulling the boy's limp body out of the pool, lifting him by the back of shirt.

Dennis laid the boy on the cold cement at the pool's edge and began administering CPR, and Frank knelt down to help.

With Frank and Dennis hovering over the motionless body, attempting to breathe life back into the child, I was left with nothing to do except watch—which is hard for most police officers to do in a life-and-death situation. Unable to help, I searched the boy's face, looking for any sign of life that might flicker there. If only *I could do something....*

Dennis continued to breathe for the boy, while Frank kept compressing his small chest, trying to get his heart going again.

My eyes fell to the coveralls that hung wet on his little body. I thought how much they looked like the ones my girls wore when they were that age. I saw the small tennis shoes on his limp feet, and noticed that one was untied. I wondered if he would ever have someone tie his shoes again.

I desperately tried to choke back the lump tightening in my throat, and could feel tears coming down my cheeks.

I turned, walked a few steps, and took out my handkerchief to wipe my eyes. As I put it back in my pocket, I saw four men standing and watching Dennis and Frank work. I recognized them as part of the group standing out front when we arrived.

I felt anger welling up inside me. "Who found the boy in the pool?" I asked.

They looked at me, but none of them said a word.

I repeated the question, surprised at how loud my voice came out. Then I continued, "Why did you just leave him in the pool? Why didn't you at least pull him out?"

They only hung their heads, and stared at the ground.

Just then the fire department arrived. Soon an oxygen mask was secured around the small face that hadn't changed expression. The firefighters took over the CPR. Dennis was still kneeling, softly stroking the boy's small, closed hand, and staring into his lifeless face....

I looked up again at the four men still standing in their group. Suddenly, as if directed by some unseen instructor, they all turned and walked out of the yard, none of them saying a word.[106]

I don't know anything else about those four men. I don't know where they worked, I don't know their ages, I don't know if they were married, and I don't know if they were Democrats or Republicans. But there's something that I do know. None of those four men was a leader. Every one of them was a follower.

Allow me to surmise something else about each of these four men. If any of them had children, my guess is that you would find them doing the same things that their fathers were doing.

Standing around.

Generally speaking, men who are followers produce children who are followers. And followers are very good at just standing around in a crisis. That little two-year-old boy lost his life because four men were followers. It's my conviction that children all over America are dying emotionally, spiritually, and morally because the men in their lives are just standing around. That's absolutely the worst thing that any man with children could ever do. Passivity is death! Whatever you do, don't stand around!

What should you do?

Sit down and write out a plan.

Set some goals for your family.

Take a successful dad out for breakfast and tap into his methods.

Get with a small group of guys and encourage and sharpen each other.

Come to one of our Men's Leadership Ministries conferences.

You'll join thousands of other men who have walked out of that conference with a plan on how to lead their families. But whatever you do, don't stand around!

I don't remember who said it, but they were right on target: "There is as much risk in doing nothing as in doing something." And doing nothing with kids in regard to leadership is simply asking for tragedy in the teenage years. Horace Bushnell once said, "Somewhere under the stars God has a job for you to do, and no one else can do it." That job, my friends, is to lead your kids by your example.

So what's it going to be, Dad? Are you standing tall...or just standing around?

Edmund Burke was right on the money: "Example is the school of mankind, and they will learn at no other."

2. Be a spiritual submarine under the surface of your children's lives.

Tom Clancy knows submarines. That why he writes the following words with such certainty:

> *Submarine.* The very word implies stealth and deadliness. Of all the conventional weapons used by the world's armed forces these days, none is more effective or dangerous than the nuclear attack submarine (SSN). Since its creation in the United States some forty years ago, the SSN has become the most feared weapon in the oceans of the world. The modern SSN is a stealth platform with 70 percent of the world's surface under which to hide, its endurance determined not by fuel but by the amount of food that may be crammed into the hull, and its operational limitations determined more by the skill of the commander and crew than by external factors....

Visually, a submarine is the least impressive of physical artifacts. Its hull does not bristle with weapons and sensors as do surface warships, and for one to see its imposing bulk, it must be in dry-dock. On those rare moments when a submarine is visible, this most lethal of ships appears no more threatening than a huge sea turtle. Yet despite that, the true capabilities of the modern SSN are most easily understood in terms of myth or the modern equivalent, a science fiction movie.

Here is a creature that, like Ridley Scott's *Alien,* appears when it wishes, destroys what it wishes, and disappears immediately to strike again when *it* wishes.[107]

May I submit to you, gentlemen, that God has called you to be an SSN for your children. When it comes to spiritual battle, you should understand that you have been given awesomely powerful weapons.

In my estimation, Ephesians 6 is telling us that godly men who are leading their families have the potential to be nothing less than the stealth warships of spiritual warfare who lurk just beneath the surface of their children's activities and affairs:

Put on the full armor of God, that you may be able to stand firm against the schemes of the devil. For our struggle is not against flesh and blood, but against rulers, against the powers, against the world forces of this darkness, against the spiritual forces of wickedness in the heavenly places. Therefore, take up the full armor of God, that you may be able to resist in the evil day, and having done everything, to stand firm. Stand firm therefore, HAVING GIRDED YOUR LOINS WITH TRUTH, AND HAVING PUT ON THE BREASTPLATE OF RIGHTEOUSNESS, and having shod YOUR FEET WITH THE PREPARATION OF THE GOSPEL OF PEACE; in addition to all, taking up the shield of faith with which you will be able to extinguish all the flaming missiles of the evil one. And take THE HELMET OF SALVATION, and sword of the Spirit, which is the word of God. With all prayer and petition pray at all times in the Spirit, and with this in view, be on the alert with all perseverance and petition for all the saints. (Ephesians 6:11–18)

A godly father is the unseen spiritual submarine who lurks below the surface of every activity in his child's life. A man who has put on the full armor of God and, with that armor, goes to warfare on his knees for his children is a force to be reckoned with. The prayers of a man who has put on the full armor of God are lethal. Effective. Protective. God responds to the prayers of such a man who is alert to pray with perseverance for his children.

We understand, gentlemen, that we cannot be with our children twenty-four hours a day. We cannot be with them every time they encounter peer pressure. You may be out of sight, but like a submarine, that does not mean you are without influence. We are in spiritual warfare. A man in the full armor of God is no less a force than an SSN. Through your prayers you have the ability to affect situations where you are not physically present. You may be undetected but that does not mean that you are ineffective.

The next five points will not take as much explanation. They're simple and direct. But don't let that fool you. They're also *strategic*.

3. Expect your children to be leaders.

"I don't know what to do," a man said to his therapist. "My wife thinks she's a piano."

"Well, then, bring her in for an appointment."

"Are you crazy?" exclaimed the husband. "Do you have any idea what it costs to move a piano?"

The moral of the story? If you *think* your kids are leaders and expect them to be leaders, then your kids will begin to see themselves as leaders.

What are your expectations? Do you expect your kids to go along with the crowd? Then they most likely will. Do you expect them to fight their way upstream when everyone else is floating with the downstream current? Then they probably will. Expect your children to be leaders. If it's important to you, it will be important to them.

4. Encourage your children to be leaders.

All leaders get discouraged. That's why they need encouragement. *Encouragement* is a great word. It means "to put courage in." That's the job of a dad. It's tough being a teenager who goes against conventional wisdom;

sometimes kids can become weary in well doing. That's especially when you must put courage in.

Two psychiatrists were at a convention. "What was your most difficult case?" one asked the other.

"Once I had a patient who lived in a pure fantasy world," replied his colleague. "He believed that a wildly rich uncle in South America was going to leave him a fortune. All day long he waited for a make-believe letter to arrive from a fictitious attorney. He never went out or did anything. He just sat around and waited."

"What was the result?"

"It was an eight-year struggle, but I finally cured him. And then that stupid letter arrived...."

The last thing we want to do is to discourage our children in any way. We don't want to discourage their dreams, their hopes, their aspirations, or their moral courage. We want to help them become optimistic about what God has in store for them to be and to do.

Thomas Fuller once said that a young trooper should have an old horse. Guess what, my friends, you are the horses. And your name isn't Trigger, Champion, or Silver. Your name had better be Encouragement.

5. Remind your children that they are leaders.

"Dad," a polar bear cub asked his father, "am I 100 percent polar bear?"

"Of course you are," answered the father bear. "My parents are 100 percent polar bear, which makes me 100 percent polar bear. Your mother's parents are 100 percent polar bear, so she's 100 percent polar bear. Yep, that makes you 100 percent polar bear. Why do you ask?"

"I'm *freezing* out here, Dad."

Kids need to be reminded frequently who they are. When I drop my kids off at school, I often say to them as they get out of the car, "Be a leader today." Why do I do that? Because they need to be reminded.

Recently I was talking to one of my boys about a particular behavior. I reminded him that our family didn't do such things. I said to him, "Papa Jim doesn't do that. Uncle Mike doesn't do that. Uncle Jeff doesn't do that. And I don't do that. Farrars don't do that, and you are a Farrar."

Young polar bears may need to be reminded who they are when they feel the cold. Our kids need to be reminded when they start following the crowd that leaders don't do that. They are *leaders,* not followers. It's your job to remind them when they begin to doubt. It was Leo Tolstoy who commented, "We lost, because we told ourselves we lost." Remind your kids that they are leaders. Frequently.

6. Support them in their leadership.

Professional golfers play every tournament round with a caddie. The caddie is more than an extra shoulder to hoist a bag of clubs. A caddie is there for support. A good caddie can be a tremendous support in the heat of competition.

Tommy Bolt was one of the greatest golfers of all time. But he had a legendary temper that almost outshone his reputation as a golfer. Tommy was playing in a tournament in Southern California one year, and he was still ticked off about his score from the day before. He told his caddie not to say a word to him.

Tommy hit his first tee shot, and it came to rest behind a tree. He asked his caddie what he thought about a five-iron. The caddie didn't reply. Tommy hit the five-iron and made an unbelievable shot that landed on the green.

Tommy turned to his caddie and said proudly, "Well, what do you think about that?"

"It wasn't your ball, Tommy," said the caddie as he picked up the bag and headed toward the green.

One of the greatest ways you can support your kids is to listen to them. When they need to talk, then you listen. When there's something eating 'em up, you find out what's going on inside their hearts. It will not be easy for your kids to be leaders when most of their friends are moral followers. And there will be times when they just need to talk. So *be there,* my friend. Be there with very large ears and a very large heart. If you do that, they will know that they are supported. Because you cared enough to listen.

This is what Ross Campbell calls "Focused Attention." Ross is a physician who has written an excellent book I have been recommending for years: *How to Really Love Your Child.*

Ross puts it this way:

What is focused attention? Focused attention is giving a child our full, undivided attention in such a way that he feels without doubt that he is completely loved. That he is valuable enough in his own right to warrant parents' undistracted watchfulness, appreciation, and uncompromising regard.[108]

Believe me, gentlemen. The child who gets focused attention will feel your complete support.

7. Reward them for demonstrating leadership.

When a child leads, he should be rewarded. When your child eats lunch at school with a kid who the other kids make fun of, he should be rewarded. When your teenager stands tall in the howling winds of peer pressure and does what is right, he should be rewarded. But how do you reward him?

When I say reward, I don't mean money, and I don't mean giving a gift. Now there is certainly a time and place for that. But there are other ways of giving a child a reward.

One of the better ways to reward your sons and daughters is with your words. Acknowledge their achievement or accomplishment verbally. There is a reason why I think this is important. When your kid does the right thing, you can count on the fact that he or she will be criticized. Criticism always follows leaders. Men and women and boys and girls who stand tall always make the easiest targets.

A young boy had practiced for years to become a great pianist. Finally the night of his debut concert arrived. The auditorium was jammed. The teenage boy played his heart out for the audience. Yet when the newspapers came out, the critics ripped apart his performance. A wise old musician put his arm around the boy and said, "Remember, young man, there is no city in the world where they have erected a statue to a critic."

Your child will have plenty of critics. Just make sure that you are not one of them. Words are very important. We all remember the childhood rhyme, "Stick and stones may break my bones, but words will never hurt me." Nothing could be further from the truth. Many of us have broken bones and have recovered very nicely in a month or so. But is it not true that we can still remember the critical words that were hurled at us on a playground twenty, thirty, forty, even fifty years ago? Words can hurt like nothing else.

Gentlemen, let's reward with our words. Samuel Goldwyn, who was the Yogi Berra of the film industry, once said of a director, "We are overpaying him, but he's worth it." When your kids demonstrate leadership, overpay them with your words.

You and I both know they're worth it.

But There Are No Guarantees

Ken Canfield makes a great point when he compares fathering to farming. There are no guarantees in either profession. A farmer can do all the right things and still lose a crop. So can a father. The farmer can till the ground at the right time, put in the right seed, and irrigate and fertilize according to the textbook. But that does not guarantee a crop.

A dad can implement all of the seven principles we've enumerated and still lose the crop. And there is nothing more heartbreaking. I'm aware of a man who, in the estimation of many godly people, has done an excellent job of cultivating his children. But recently one of his teenage daughters became pregnant.

Gentlemen, it could happen to any of us. All we can do is the best we can do. Perhaps you have a hard time understanding how a man could be such an outstanding leader and have one of his kids fail morally. The answer is that our kids are still kids. Because of circumstances, peer pressure, and lack of experience, they will make some choices at times that will not be the choices we had hoped for. Just like we did when we were their age.

My point in writing this chapter is not to say that we can be such great fathers as to guarantee that our kids will exhibit spiritual leadership in every situation they face. They won't, because they are human. But I am writing to say that the farmer who tills the soil, plants good seed, and irrigates his crop has a much better hope for a good crop than the man who doesn't plant any seed to begin with.

But there are no guarantees. I have the ability to make choices and so do my kids. And if God has blessed your life with kids that have—up to now—made the right choices, then be careful. Be grateful but also be careful.

In September 1985 a party was held at one of the largest city pools in New Orleans. The reason for the festive occasion? The summer of 1985 was the first summer in years that a drowning did not occur at a New Orleans city pool. The summer was now officially over, and two hundred guests were at the celebration, including over one hundred certified lifeguards.

It was a great party! All were thrilled at the accomplishment of the summer. It wasn't until the party was over that they noticed the fully clothed man at the bottom of the pool near the drain. They attempted to revive him, but it was too late. The man had drowned, surrounded by lifeguards who were celebrating their success.

God has been good to many of us with our kids. But before we get carried away celebrating our successes, let's not forget to stay on our knees.

Let me say a word to those of you who may have had a tough time with this chapter. You have a child who is not responding to the principles you have carefully instilled into his or her life. Perhaps your teenager has recently made a choice that has apparently torpedoed much of what you had hoped and dreamed for that young life. Don't lose heart, my friend. You may be thinking that the crop you have worked and hoped for in the life of your son or daughter may never come in.

That's how the father of the Prodigal Son must have felt for quite a while. There had to be nights when he felt that the crop he had hoped to reap in the life of his son was lost forever.

But it ain't over until it's over.

Prodigals have a way of coming home. That's why you might want to keep a fatted calf ready. Or at least a few extra steaks in the freezer. You never know when that crop might pull into the driveway.

WALKING TALL

1. Do you find yourself moved or convicted by Officer Dave Johnson's story of the four men who "just stood around," instead of pulling the little boy out of the pool? When it comes to being a spiritual leader in your home, do you ever feel as though you're doing a lot of standing around? How has this book helped or encouraged you to break that pattern?

2. Take a moment to review the following scriptures: Ephesians 6:18, Philippians 4:6–7, Colossians 4:2, 12–13, and James 5:16. As you consider the implications of fighting spiritual battles in your child's life, look again at Colossians 4:12–13. Describe the kind of prayer ministry a guy named Epaphras was having in the lives of the Colossian believers. What do you think it means to "labor earnestly" (NASB) or "wrestle" (NIV) for someone in prayer? What kind of impact could that kind of prayer— coming from you, their dad—have in the lives of your kids through the years? Is it a ministry you've seriously considered before now? How can we as men encourage one another in this crucial area of helping our kids stand tall?

3. Consider again Dr. Ross Campbell's explanation of supporting your child through focused attention:

    > Focused attention is giving a child our full, undivided attention in such a way that he feels without doubt that he is completely loved. That he is valuable enough in his own right to warrant his parents' undistracted watchfulness, appreciation, and uncompromising regard.

    As you look back over the last couple of weeks, have you been giving each of your kids the benefit of such attention? What are some ways a man might remind himself to carve out some focused time for each child during the course of a week?

4. Take a three-by-five-inch card and write out the seven steps I've outlined in this chapter. If you're serious about helping your sons and daughters stand tall, stick the card someplace where your eyes will fall on it every day. Tape it to the bathroom mirror where you shave, or tape it to the dashboard of your car. It could provide some stimulating conversation in the old car pool!

11

WOMENFOLK

*I don't mind living in a man's world as
long as I can be a woman in it.*
SUSAN BARKELY

I have never been tortured.

But I still remember the day I had an impacted wisdom tooth removed. In my mind, there seems to be a direct correlation between the two experiences. They put me out to remove the tooth, so I really don't know how they got it out. But the way my jaw felt I suspect they blasted it out.

That's why I was up that night at 2:30 A.M. And that's why I was watching an old episode of *Rawhide*. That show was one of the great TV westerns. Even though I was in pain, it brought back good memories to watch Gil Favor, Rowdy Yates, and Wishbone.

That night, Gil and Rowdy rode into town to find some of the boys who got drunk at the saloon. As I watched them walk through town, I began to notice something about the way they interacted with people. Every time they would pass by a woman, they would tip their hats. When they addressed a woman, they called her "ma'am." These two rough-and-tumble trail drivers were very careful with their manners when it came to "womenfolk."

What struck me about these cowboys was that they were *respectful* of women. That's the way real men would relate to "womenfolk" in the Old West. And real men do the same thing today.

One of the telltale signs of our rapid national erosion is the way women are treated in our land. To put it on the table, we are developing into a nation where women are not respected. And the flaw has been in the moral fabric for quite a while.

I'll never forget the first time an abused woman walked into my office. I hadn't been pastoring long, and I wasn't happy with the way she had been treated. Her eye was bruised, and her lip was split and broken. After I talked with her and got her some medical attention, I drove down to her husband's place of employment.

This guy sold new cars. As I walked into the showroom, I could tell he was a little surprised to see me.

I walked up to him and said, "I'd like to make a deal with you."

So we went into one of those little white offices and sat down, just like we were going to negotiate on a car. But I wasn't there to talk about a car.

"Let me offer you a deal," I told him. "The next time you decide you want to hit somebody, I want you to call me up. I'll come over to your house, and you can hit me and I won't hit you back. That's the deal. But if you ever strike your wife again, our elder board will press charges against you faster than you can believe."

This guy was pretty rough with a woman. That's why he wasn't a real man. Real men don't strike women. But unless I miss my guess, the reason this guy hit women was because he was raised in a home where women were struck. In other words, he didn't know how to respect a woman because his father never *taught* him to respect women.

Gentlemen, if you would like to make a difference in this nation, let me suggest to you that you teach your sons to respect women. Our country is crying out for men who know how to treat women in a biblical and gracious manner.

A commentary from Chuck Colson underscores the need for such behavior from young men in a culture that has lost its moral mind. According to Colson, there is a new fad going on in public swimming pools in New York City. It's called "whirlpooling." Colson writes:

> Twenty to thirty boys link arms in a circle and surround a solitary girl. The boys close in on her, dunk her head under water, and frequently tear off her bathing suit and grab at her.
>
> The problem has grown so severe that in New York City several teenage boys have actually been arrested. Some girls say they're afraid to go to the pool alone....
>
> The underlying philosophy that spawns this ugliness was uncovered in an informal survey by the *New York Times*. Reporters asked several teens how they accounted for the boys' predatory behavior in the swimming pools.
>
> "It's nature," one boy replied. "Look at a female dog and a male dog. It's the same thing: you see 20 male dogs on a female dog. It's the male nature, in a way."
>
> How utterly repugnant. But how utterly consistent with what these kids are being taught in public schools. The great prophet of sex education was Alfred Kinsey, who built his theory of sexuality squarely on the foundation of scientific naturalism. Humans are part of nature, Kinsey taught—nothing more....
>
> The Bible does not teach that we are mere dogs in heat. It teaches that we are bearers of the image of God.[109]

I don't know any more details about "whirlpooling" than what Colson reported. But there are two things that come to mind. First, I would have liked to see Gil Favor and Rowdy Yates show up at that swimming pool. And secondly, none of those boys who were in involved in such a sick activity were taught by their fathers to respect women.

Women are not being respected in our culture. It's just another sign of the moral and spiritual sickness that plagues our nation. Women are hit, raped, abused, grabbed, and harassed. Is there anything we can do about this problem that plagues us? Yes, there is. We can teach our sons *early* to respect women.

Just think about the problem and its root causes. They all go back to the home.

- Men who strike women were not taught to respect women.
- Men who rape women were not taught to respect women.
- Men who divorce their wives for younger women were not taught to respect women.
- Men who sexually harass women with crass innuendoes were not taught to respect women.
- Men who don't live with their wives in an understanding way were not taught to respect women.
- Men who don't grant their wives honor as a fellow heir of the grace of life were not taught to respect women.

Now the key question is this: When in his life does a man learn to respect women? The answer is that a man should learn to respect a woman when he is a boy. *And he should learn it from his father.*

My wife told me recently of a situation that she witnessed between a ten-year-old boy and his mother. It should also be pointed out that the boy's father had just left his mother for another woman. It was a public setting, and the woman asked the boy to get his things so that they could get into the car and go pick up his younger brother.

"I'll go when I'm ready," said the boy.

"We have to go now," said the mother.

"Shut up," retorted the boy.

"Don't talk to me that way!"

"I'll talk to you any way I want to," said the boy as he stalked off.

The mother, who had just been through the humiliation of having her husband leave her for a younger woman, was now publicly embarrassed by a ten-year-old who was completely out of control. She stood in a group of observant adults, deeply humiliated by a boy who was emulating the example of his dad. Like father, like son.

Last summer my wife and I were invited to speak at the Christian Business Men's Committee national convention in Orlando. The hotel was right next door to Disney World, and we had a great time with our family that week. Our sessions were in the morning, so we were free in the afternoons and evenings to go to Disney World.

I was committed for an evening meeting on Tuesday, so I left Mary and the kids at Epcot and went back to the conference. Mary recounted an interesting experience she had when they returned to the hotel. As they came into the lobby at about 10:00 P.M., Mary asked one of our boys to go to the coffee shop with the rest of the group, while Mary dropped some packages in the hotel room.

"Mom, can I go find Dad?" he asked.

"No, I want everyone to stay together. You stay with the kids and go to the coffee shop. I'll be right there, and Dad is planning on meeting us there."

"Yes, ma'am," he said.

As Mary got into the elevator a lady got in with her.

"I want you to know that I was very impressed with your son back there," she said.

"Oh, really?" replied Mary.

"We have been at Disney World all week, and it seems that all I have seen this week are children who don't know how to obey their parents. All week long I have had my fill of spoiled kids arguing with their parents in the most abusive terms when they didn't get their way. It was absolutely refreshing to see a boy who knew how to obey his mother."

Now that is quite a social commentary. Please don't get the idea that things always work that way at our house. I could enumerate a number of stories where the outcome of the discussion wasn't resolved as it was that evening. But the point here is that a watching stranger found my son's simple obedience to his mother so *unusual* that she felt compelled to comment on it. That is a very sad commentary.

One of the key times in the life of boys and girls is adolescence. This is often the time when the parameters are tested. And this is often the time when a wrong pattern of acting disrespectfully takes root. As a boy grows in physical stature, it becomes quite tempting to try his wings with his newfound size and physical strength. This is precisely where the respect for a mother will be tested. The reason I know this is that I remember being thirteen years old. In twelve months' time, I grew from five feet seven inches and 130 pounds to six feet three inches and 190 pounds. Believe me, I was feeling my oats.

I can remember a talk I had with my dad like it was yesterday afternoon. The topic of our conversation was my tone of voice and the content of my speech to my mother. I may have been impressed with my newfound size, but my dad wasn't impressed in the least. He wouldn't have been impressed if I had been seven feet three inches. You see, I was impressed with physical size. My dad was impressed with the size of character and attitude. And the purpose of our discussion was to cut me down to size.

What size did my dad whittle me down to? He brought me down to the reality that no matter how tall I was, or how much I weighed, or how old I was, I was *under* the authority of my mother. He reminded me that this wasn't between me and my mother. It was between me and him.

I recently came across a "Calvin and Hobbes" cartoon that captures the idea. Calvin says to Hobbes, "I feel bad that I called Susie names and hurt her feelings. I'm sorry I did it."

"Maybe you should apologize to her," Hobbes suggests.

Calvin thinks about this momentarily and then retorts, "I keep hoping there's a less obvious solution."

I had to laugh recently when a friend of mine had a similar encounter with his soon-to-be-thirteen-year-old boy. The boy was starting to display some very disrespectful behavior to his mother. My friend made it clear to him that this was not going to continue. The boy would do well for a while...and then he would get upset and start running off his mouth to his mother.

The father was getting ready to go on a business trip for a couple of days. He sat down and talked with his son and reminded him that he fully expected him to speak respectfully to his mother while he was away. If he did not, there would be certain severe consequences upon his return. The first night away the dad called the son, and in the course of their conversation, he reminded him about his expectation of his behavior.

The next night that dad got in from the airport at about 10:30 P.M. As he walked in the door, his wife looked very discouraged. She proceeded to tell him about the latest bout of disrespect. The dad listened, took his suitcase upstairs, and went into his son's bedroom. He got the boy out of bed, and they went into the family room to talk. He went back over his instructions. The boy agreed that he understood the instructions.

The father then commenced to apply knowledge to the seat of understanding. But he was not through. He was just beginning. He then told his son that he was at a crossroads. A very important crossroads. He explained to the son that it was his desire for his son to enjoy life. But it was the boy's decision whether or not that would happen.

The father was very direct in explaining to his son that another verbal barrage on his mother would mean that his choice had been made. One more bout of disrespect would mean that the boy was done with football and done with all social activities at school. This father wasn't kidding around. A man who respects his wife protects his wife.

Fortunately, this dad had a large amount of credibility capital with his son. The boy knew his dad meant every word. He knew that his father would pull him off the football team without even thinking twice. His father reminded him that football and social activities were privileges that were earned. They were not rights. The father then reminded the son that this was not an issue between the boy and the mother, but between him and his boy. He also let the boy know that it was the boy who would make the choice of living a miserable existence. If there was one more episode, football was over in mid-September.

Over the next few weeks there was an amazing transformation of character. The boy suddenly became very careful of his speech. He seemed to work overtime to be kind and loving to his mother. Why was the boy suddenly motivated to bring about such a change in character?

I believe the term is known as *fear*.

And just as the fear of the heavenly Father is the beginning of wisdom, so the fear of an earthly father is also the beginning of wisdom.

One thing needs to be pointed out. This father loves his son deeply. He loves his son more than words could ever express. He is committed to seeing his son live a full, productive, and meaningful life. This father wants his son to have a good marriage and great relationships with his children. Those are the motives behind the father's remarks.

One more thing. It was all the father could do to keep from laughing when he was talking with his son. Because he kept remembering a similar talk his father had with him when he was approximately the same age. When he heard himself using some of the exact words and phrases that his father had used with him more than thirty years prior, it was all he could do to keep a straight face. And thirty or so years in the future, his son will also have to work very hard to keep a straight face when he repeats those same phrases to his boy.

There's yet another interesting twist to this story. Weeks later, this man was talking to his wife about the remarkable character transformation in the life of their son. Now the boy hadn't become perfect, but when he started to slip into disrespect he would catch himself and quickly shift attitudinal gears.

That's when the wife said, "In all of our years of marriage you have done some wonderful things for me. You have given me wonderful gifts, and we have taken some very special trips. But nothing you have ever done for me has meant more to me than the way that you demanded that our son respect me. You will never know how that let me know how much you love me and value me."

Whoa! This guy was completely blown away. He couldn't believe the impact that his actions had had on his wife, as well as on his son.

Gentlemen, this is what you call male leadership. This is the solution to the sexual harassment problem, the rape problem, the physical abuse problem, and a few other problems that we probably haven't even thought about. Let me put it another way. Boys who love and respect their mothers don't abuse women, and they don't rape women. But you take away the respect from an adolescent boy and you are asking for trouble that will affect all of society.

In George Bernard Shaw's *Pygmalion,* Eliza Doolittle married Freddy Eynsford-Hill because she knew that she would always be a cockney flower girl to Professor Henry Higgins. She knew that he could never accept the change in her, but would always see her as she used to be. As she told Freddy, "The difference between a lady and a flower girl is not how she behaves but how she's treated. I shall always be a flower girl to Professor Higgins because he always treats me as a flower girl and always will; but I know I can be a lady to you because you always treat me like a lady and always will."[110]

I realize that there are cases when an innocent man is accused of sexual impropriety and there is nothing to the allegations. But I am not speaking of such cases. My comments are directed to the situations where women are taken advantage of by men. The time to cure an irresponsible man who doesn't know how to treat a woman respectfully is not at age thirty or forty or fifty. It is at twelve or thirteen. Quite frankly, gentlemen, anything past that is too late.

The mighty Niagara river plummets some 180 feet at the American and Horseshoe Falls. Before the falls, there are violent, turbulent rapids. Farther upstream, however, where the river's current flows more gently, boats are able to navigate. Just before the Welland River empties into the Niagara, a pedestrian walkway spans the river. Posted on this bridge's pylons is a warning sign for all boaters: DO YOU HAVE AN ANCHOR? DO YOU KNOW HOW TO USE IT?[111]

There is a place on the Niagara River that symbolizes the point of no return. There is a time in the lives of our children where they, too, will be caught up in an irresistible current. That current is a combination of adolescent experimentation and cultural attitudes to God-ordained authority that—if left unchallenged—will sweep our children over the falls to a life of relational chaos. They will *drown* in those wrong attitudes. Not only will they drown, but they will take others with them.

Do you want to do something to stop the moral deterioration of our nation? Then anchor your son.

A father is the anchor that God has placed in the life of a child. It is the father's role and responsibility to dig deeply into the solid rock of Christ in order to tether a young boy headed in the wrong direction. Every boy needs the bone-jarring yank that occurs when the anchor takes hold.

That yank of a loving father has kept many a boy from going over the falls. And the astonishing thing about that fact is this: That yank on the life of your boy won't save just him. An anchor that holds that deeply into the bedrock of Christ will save not only your boy, but also *his* boy, and *his* boy. Real men yank on the chain of the generations and demand respect for women.

And here's the deal on this chain. It's real long and it's real strong. It goes way back, further than you may have imagined. For on the other end of the anchor is the One who in His last moments on the cross thought not of himself, but of a woman, and entrusted her care into the hands of a trusted friend. He not only died for His mother, but also He respected His mother. And we can do no less than to uphold His example of ideal masculinity for our families.

The term *womenfolk* may be outdated, but the term *respect* is not. For godly men it is still very much in vogue.

Drop the anchor, my friends, and pull hard on the chain. You will save your family from sure disaster.

WALKING TALL

1. What does it mean to treat a woman in a "biblical" way? Take a few minutes to consider the following scriptures: John 19:25–27; 1 Timothy 5:1–2; 1 Peter 3:7; Ephesians 5:25–30, 33; Colossians 3:19. Looking through a wide-angle lens, what are some of the main attitudes and actions conveyed by these biblical writers?

2. Now, looking through a zoom lens, focus in on 1 Peter 3:7, and then verses 8 and 9 following. Summarize Peter's thoughts in your own words. Talk about the impact on your sons and daughters as they see you living with your wife in the way Peter describes.

3. To what degree have you seen your attitude toward your wife reflected in your son or daughter's attitude toward his or her mother? In what way would you like to see that reflection improve or change?

12

OUTPOSTS OF CIVILIZATION

*We act as though it were our mission to bring about
the triumph of truth, but our mission is only to fight for it.*

BLAISE PASCAL

A TV news camera crew was on assignment in southern Florida filming the widespread destruction from Hurricane Andrew. In one scene, amid the devastation and debris, stood one house on its foundation. The owner was cleaning up the yard when a reporter approached him.

"Sir, why is your house the only one in the entire neighborhood that is standing?" asked the reporter. "How did you manage to escape the severe damage of the hurricane?"

"I built this house myself," the man replied. "I also built it according to the Florida state building code. When the code called for two-by-six roof trusses, I used two-by-six roof trusses. I was told that a house built according to code could withstand a hurricane. I did and it did. I suppose no one else around here followed the code."[112]

A house built to the moral code of Scripture can also withstand a *moral* hurricane. And that's what we are in, gentlemen. A hurricane. We should remember that as bad as hurricanes can be, some houses remain standing. But the house must be built according to code.

Most men don't take the time or effort to build according to code. They would rather take the shortcuts. But your shortcuts will find you out! Just ask the people who lost their homes in Hurricane Andrew. In that entire neighborhood, only one house remained standing. And it was the house of a man who built it himself according to the predetermined standards of the code. He didn't do what everyone else did. In fact, he did what everyone else *didn't* do. When all else fails, read the directions. Oh yeah, there's one more thing. Don't just don't read the directions. *Follow* the directions.

Just because we are in the hurricane doesn't mean that we have to be pessimistic. Some people are negative all the time. One guy described his outlook on life with this statement, "I was going to read a book on positive thinking. But then I thought, *What good will do that do?*" That's certainly not the Christian perspective.

I like the perspective characterized by a good ol' boy from the backwoods by the name of Jeb. Wolves were picking off the livestock of ranchers at an alarming rate, so the state offered a bounty of five thousand dollars for every wolf killed. Jeb and his friend Ernie decided to go into the wolf hunting business. They had been out huntin' wolves all day and into the night and made camp way up in the mountains near a beautiful little stream. About four o' clock in the morning, Jeb woke up to see their camp surrounded by thirty or forty wolves. In the light of the dying campfire, he could see the blood lust in their eyes and the white of their exposed, razor-sharp teeth. He could also see that they were about ready to spring.

"Hey, Ernie," he whispered. "Wake up! *We're rich!*"

Now that's a man with a positive attitude.

Guys, as we look at what's happening around us, we should understand that we are rich. Rich with opportunity, that is. The early days of America were no piece of cake. Building a new nation with new opportunity meant plenty of risk. It meant putting yourself on the line. Men died for the freedoms we enjoy today, just as they have done at various times in our two hundred–year history. It was in those early days of great risk and uncertainty that Abigail

Adams wrote a letter to Thomas Jefferson. In that letter, dated 1790, Mrs. Adams had a bit of wisdom for the ages.

She wrote: "These are the hard times in which a genius would wish to live. Great necessities call forth great leaders."

Abigail Adams took a long look at the world around her and saw it brimming with threats and difficulties. And she realized she was rich. That woman was a leader.

Gentlemen, we are living in days of great necessities. That's why you're rich. For you have an opportunity to offer great leadership to your family. Who is the man who is the great leader? It is the man who builds his family according to code.

There was another time in history when there were great necessities. After the fall of the Roman Empire, things were so bad historians have called that period the Dark Ages. The great empire fell to ravaging, marauding bands from the east over a period of approximately fifty years. Society as it had been known broke down.

But here and there were pockets of civility in the midst of barbarism.

Why was there civility? Because some folks were building according to code.

There was a group of men who stood against the culture and infiltrated the culture, and eventually they changed the culture. Even though things were dark, they believed in the light of the gospel. It not only made a difference in their lives, but also in the lives of all whom they touched.

In the fifth century it appeared that Western Europe was headed for nothing less than total barbarism. As Charles Colson so brilliantly described in his book *Against the Night,* only one force prevented barbarism from taking Europe. And that force was the church. Allow me to quote from Colson and then draw a parallel to where we are today in America.

> Instead of conforming to the barbarian culture of the Dark Ages, the medieval church modeled a counterculture to a world engulfed by destruction and confusion. Thousands of monastic orders spread across Europe, characterized by discipline, creativity, and a coherence and moral order lacking in the world around them. Monks preserved not only the Scriptures but classical literature as well; they were busy

not only at their prayers but in clearing land, building towns, and harvesting crops. When little else shone forth, these religious communities provided attractive models of communities of caring and character, and in the process they preserved both faith and civilization itself...by holding on to such vestiges of civilization—faith, learning, and civility—these monks and nuns held back the night, and eventually the West emerged from the Dark Ages into a renewed period of cultural creativity, education, and art. The barbarians could not withstand this stubborn preservation of culture.[113]

The monks preserved Christian civilization in a dark age by building little outposts of civilization across Europe. And when they built their outposts, they built them according to the code.

As we have seen, we live in a culture that contains powerful groups hellbent on removing every vestige of the Bible from our society. You recall that earlier we cited an incredible event where common sense was assassinated. A convicted murderer's sentence to life in prison was revoked because one of the attorneys quoted a phrase from the Bible in his closing argument. He didn't even quote a verse; it was just a phrase. I think that most of us by now would agree that our civilization is seriously lacking in one attribute. That attribute is *civilization.*

Now my question is this: We are living in an age growing darker by the day. Who is going to preserve the message of the Scriptures as the monks did in their little groups during the first Dark Ages?

The answer is that Christian men are going to do it.

Christian men are going to emphasize the Scriptures in the enclaves of their own homes even as the culture attempts to eradicate the Bible from the life of our nation. For that is how civilization is kept within civilization. Our job is the same as the monks. We are to build outposts of civilization. And we are to build them according to code.

Those little monastic orders were the instruments God used to preserve His truth. He wants to do the same thing in this culture with your family and my family, for the family is the church in miniature.

In those little outposts:

- God's Word was read and obeyed.
- Prayer was a source of focus and encouragement.
- Women were respected.
- Leaders were developed.
- Morality was practiced.
- Discipline was expected.
- Accountability was the order of the day.

Gentlemen, those same factors must characterize our families. May I suggest to you that this is how a man disciples his children? He raises them in a family that is an outpost of civilization. And the father makes sure that the outpost is built according to code.

Where is the code found? It is found in various parts of the Scriptures, but you can get right to the essence of it in Deuteronomy 6. Note how Moses addresses the men of Israel:

> Now this is the commandment, the statutes and the judgments which the LORD your God has commanded me to teach you, that you might do them in the land where you are going over to possess it, so that you and your son and your grandson might fear the LORD your God, to keep all His statutes and His commandments, which I command you, all the days of your life, and that your days may be prolonged. O Israel, you should listen and be careful to do it, that it may be well with you and that you may multiply greatly, just as the LORD, the God of your fathers, has promised you, in a land flowing with milk and honey.
>
> Hear, O Israel! The LORD is our God, the LORD is one! And you shall love the LORD your God with all your heart and with all your soul and with all your might. And these words, which I am commanding you today, shall be on your heart; and you shall teach them diligently to your sons and shall talk of them when you sit in your house and when you walk by the way and when you lie down and when you rise up. (Deuteronomy 6:1–7)

THE BOTTOM LINE

Out of Moses' instruction to the men of Israel, I see that the code prescribes two ironclad essentials for discipling your children.

- A man is to be with his children.
- A man is to teach his children.

When you stop and think about it, this is precisely how Jesus discipled the Twelve. He was with them and He taught them.

We're all fighting a battle for enough family time. Everyone is busy, and it seems that we are going in three directions at once. So the first question is this: How are you doing in the "with" category? For you see, if you are going to build according to code, there has to be time just to be "with."

A number of years ago, Dr. Robert Schuller was on a whirlwind book promotion tour, visiting eight cities in four days. It was an exhausting schedule in addition to the normal duties that Dr. Schuller had on his shoulders as pastor of a large church. As he was going over his schedule with his secretary for his return home, she reminded him that he was scheduled to have lunch with the winner of a charity raffle. Tickets had been raffled for a lunch with Dr. Schuller. Schuller was suddenly sobered when he found out the winner of the raffle, for he happened to know that the five hundred dollars the person bid to have lunch with him represented that person's entire life savings.

How did he know that?

The person who was willing to spend five hundred dollars to have lunch with Dr. Schuller was his own teenage daughter.

Dr. Schuller obviously loves his family as much as any of us do. He graciously allowed Paul Harvey to tell this story in his column. It simply reminds us fathers that we can be so busy doing what is good that we forget what is of real importance. So many of the things we believe are "caught" by our kids when they are "with" us. That's the value of time.

According to the code, the second task is to *teach*. Guys, let me shoot absolutely straight with you. This is so basic and fundamental that the tendency—the very strong tendency—would be to put this book down.

But I have a question for you: Whose job is it to teach your kids the Scriptures? The Sunday school teacher, the youth pastor, the pastor?

According to Deuteronomy 6, it's *your* job. And no one has been a bigger failure at this than me.

For years, we never had a consistent family devotional time during the week. From time to time I'd take a stab at it—only to watch my kids' eyes glaze over and roll back in their heads. But about a year ago I woke up and realized what was going on. My kids are being raised in a Baal-like culture. If I don't give them the Word of God, then no one will give them the Word of God. Sure, they'll get it at Sunday school, but guys, forty-five minutes in Sunday school is not going to counterbalance the Baal-possessed culture that they function in the other six and a half days.

Let me tell you what I stumbled across. It's a plan that's so simple it's absolutely profound. About a year and a half ago, Mary suggested to me that as a family, we read the Bible together.

That's it?

That's it.

We make sure the homework is done and the TV is off. Any dad in the world can lead his family spiritually by turning off the TV and getting everyone together in the family room. Everyone opens his or her Bible, and we start reading. We read right through a book. We've read through Esther, Ruth, 1 Kings, and a bunch of other books. I look at the chapter and see how many verses there are. Then I divide the chapter into thirds (because I have three kids) and let each take his or her turn reading.

If your kids are small and can't read, then you should get them *The Beginner's Bible.*[114] Kids absolutely go crazy over *The Beginner's Bible.* It's at their level of understanding so that when Dad reads to them they won't fall asleep. It's also a great first Bible for a child just learning to read.

Our kids are older, so we vary from a regular Bible translation to *The Wonder Bible.*[115] *The Wonder Bible* is a great tool for kids between eight and twelve. It summarizes everything in the Scriptures without compromising the essence and makes for a much easier read for kids. Each of our kids has a *Wonder Bible.* It's a great tool. Of course, as your kids grow older, they can begin reading directly from the Scriptures.

We don't do this every night because life is nuts! But we shoot for two to three nights a week. We read the Word, and then sometimes we have great discussions and other nights we don't. That will take care of itself.

Any guy in the world can do this. If your kids ask you a question that you don't know, then *tell* them you don't know. That's no disgrace! But make sure you follow up and get back to them. If you get stuck, give your pastor a call. He'll be more than happy to help a man who is leading his family in the study of God's Word.

Guys, let me tell you why this is so important. Note what Moses said to the men of Israel about their job of building their outpost of civilization according to code: "So the LORD commanded us to observe all these statutes, to fear the LORD our God for our good always *and for our survival,* as it is today" (Deuteronomy 6:24, emphasis mine).

Did you catch that?

It is for our SURVIVAL.

Moses knew that Israel was going into Canaan. But guess who was waiting in Canaan? Baal was in Canaan, waiting to swallow the families of Israel that didn't have a man at the helm who was smart enough to build his outpost according to code.

Hey, guys, Baal worship is everywhere in this country. How in the world are your kids ever going to learn to filter the demonic teaching and thinking that barrages them twenty-four hours a day? Their only hope for survival is that you give them the Word of God. With the Word of God, they will be able to filter out the lies of the culture. And as they watch you love your Lord, love your wife, and take a stand for truth in this culture, believe me, they are going to put the pieces together.

Baal has invaded our land as he once invaded Israel. Alasdair MacIntyre has pondered our secular situation and reached this conclusion:

> If my account of our moral condition is correct, we ought to conclude that for some time now we too have reached the turning point. What matters at this stage is the construction of local forms of community with which civility and the intellectual and moral life can be sustained through the new dark ages which are already upon us. And if the tradition of the virtues was able to survive the horrors of the last dark ages, we are not entirely without grounds for hope.

He's talking about building an outpost of civilization. But guys, it will only stand if it's built to the standards of the code. The only way to do that is to put the Bible back in the central place of your home. You must read the Scriptures personally and then read them to your children. For without the Scriptures, our culture has no hope and your children have no hope. If your children are not schooled in the Scriptures, then how will they maintain the truth to pass on to their children?

Generations of the past knew this. Allan Bloom describes the way it used to be:

> It was the home (and the houses of worship related to it) where religion lived. The holy days and the common language and set of references that permeated most households constituted a large part of the family bond and gave it a substantial content. Moses and the Table of the Law, Jesus and his preaching of brotherly love, had an imaginative existence. Passages from the Psalms and the Gospels echoed in children's heads. Attending church or synagogue, praying at the table, were a way of life, inseparable from the moral education that supposed to be the family's special responsibility in this democracy. Actually, the moral teaching was the religious teaching. There was no abstract doctrine. The things one was supposed to do, the sense that the world supported them and punished disobedience, were all incarnated in the Biblical stories. The loss of the gripping inner life vouchsafed those who were nurtured by the Bible must be primarily attributed not to our schools or political life, but to the family, which, with all its rights to privacy, has proved unable to maintain any content of its own. *The dreariness of the family's spiritual landscape passes belief.* It is as monochrome and unrelated to those who pass through it as are the barren steppes frequented by nomads who take their mere substance and move on. The delicate fabric of the civilization into which the successive generations are woven has unraveled, and children are raised, not educated.

> I am speaking here not of the unhappy, broken homes that are such a prominent part of American life, but the relatively happy ones,

where husband and wife like each other and care about their children, very often unselfishly devoting the best parts of their lives to them. But they have nothing to give their children in the way of a vision of the world, of high models of action or profound sense of connection with others. The family requires the most delicate mixture of nature and convention, of human and divine, to subsist and perform its function. Its base is merely bodily reproduction, but its purpose is the formation of civilized human beings. In teaching a language and providing names for all things, it transmits an interpretation of the order of the whole of things. It feeds on books, in which the little polity—the family—believes, which tell about right and wrong, good and bad, and explain why they are so. The family requires a certain authority and wisdom about the ways of the heavens and of men. The parents must have knowledge of what has happened in the past, and prescriptions for what ought to be, in order to resist the philistinism or the wickedness of the present.... The family, however, has to be a sacred unity believing in the permanence of what it teaches, if its ritual and ceremony are to express and transmit the wonders of the moral law, which it alone is capable of transmitting and which makes it special in a world devoted to the humanly, all too humanly, useful. When that belief disappears, as it has, the family has, at best, a transitory togetherness. People sup together, travel together, but they do not think together. Hardly any homes have any intellectual life whatsoever, let alone one that informs the vital interests of life. Educational TV marks the high tide for family intellectual life.[116]

I was driving home one night and a song came on the radio that I had never heard before. It was so profound, I tracked down the lyrics the next afternoon.

> *Grandpa, tell me 'bout the good old days,*
> *Sometimes it feels like this world's gone crazy.*
> *Grandpa, take me back to yesterday.*
> *When the line between right and wrong didn't seem so hazy.*
> *Did lovers really fall in love to stay,*

Stand beside each other come what may?
A promise really something people kept,
Not just something they would say,
And then forget?
Did families really bow their heads to pray?
Daddies really never go away?
Grandpa, tell me 'bout the good old days.[117]

Gentlemen, our kids don't need to be told about the good old days. They need to be *shown* the good old days. And the one to show them is you. In your home.

There are no shortcuts to building your outpost of civilization. But quite frankly, it really isn't that difficult. If you will take the time to turn off your in-house direct link to the nightly network feed of Baal thinking, God will make a difference in your family. In turn your family will be able to make a difference in some other family that's following Baal—even though they don't know who he is.

Just as the monks brought light and hope and civility to their troubled and dark times, may I suggest today that God desires to use Christian churches and families in the same way? As we stand tall and lead and love our families in the midst of a culture growing weaker by the day, may history one day look upon us and perhaps describe us in the following manner:

Instead of conforming to the barbarian culture of moral relativism, the Christian church and family in the 1990s modeled a counterculture to a world engulfed by moral destruction and confusion. Thousands of Christian families were found across America, and they were characterized by discipline, creativity, and a coherence and moral order lacking in the culture around them. Christian fathers preserved the Scriptures by reading the Word of God to their families and introducing them to the collective wisdom of its pages. Christian families were busy, but not too busy to meet most evenings for the reading of Scripture and prayer. But they also worked hard in their appointed tasks and contributed to society by doing so. When little else shone forth, these Christian families, led by Christian fathers and husbands, provided attractive models of communities of caring and character. In the process, they preserved both faith and civilization itself. By holding on to such vestiges of civilization—faith, learning, and civility—these Christian husbands and wives and single parents held back the night. Eventually, America emerged from the Dark Ages of moral relativism as revival swept the land. This launched the nation into a renewed period of cultural creativity, education, and art that reflected their trust and confidence in a holy and sovereign God.

If you will build according to the code, your house will be standing when the others are in shambles. And they will notice, and they will ask you what you did. And you can show them the code and introduce them to the One who wrote the code.

LORD OF LORDS

In the New Testament, Baal is known as Beelzebul, which literally means "Lord of the House." In Matthew 12:24–27, Jesus clearly identifies Beelzebul (Baal) as Satan.

Gentlemen, every house has a "lord." That's why Joshua was so emphatic to state "As for me and my house, we will serve the LORD" (Joshua 24:15).

There are many homes in this nation that have become outposts of Baal. He has deceived them and he ultimately is directing them. These homes of Baal desperately need to see the truth of the Lord of lords. Satan (Baal) is the great deceiver. Do you remember that one of the names of Baal was "Rider of the Clouds"? That term came from an ancient poem about Baal that hit the charts in Elijah's day. The poem literally reads:

Seven years shall Baal,
Eight the Rider of the Clouds,
No Dew, No Rain,
No welling up of the deep,
No sweetness of Baal's voice.[118]

Baal, you'll remember, was widely thought to control the weather and the rainfall. This poem, which was known in the households of Baal, taught that Baal controlled the rain and even the dew!

But Elijah knew this was a fraud. When Elijah showed up for the first time before Ahab, he specifically said, "As the LORD, the God of Israel lives, before whom I stand, surely there shall be *neither dew nor rain* these years, except by my word" (1 Kings 17:1, emphasis mine).

Elijah walked right into a household of Baal and spoke the real truth. Baal doesn't control the dew and rain. The God of Israel controls the dew and the rain. Satan has always been a deceiver of households and families. No wonder he had the gall to refer to Baal as the "The Rider of the Clouds."

Baal is not the rider of the clouds. The Lord Jesus Christ is the Rider of the Clouds:

> And I saw heaven opened; and behold, a white horse, and He who sat upon it is called Faithful and True; and in righteousness He judges and wages war. And His eyes are a flame of fire, and upon His Head are many diadems; and He has a name written upon Him which no one knows except Himself. And He is clothed with a robe dipped in blood; and His name is called The Word of God. And the armies which are in heaven, clothed in fine linen, white and clean, were following Him on white horses. And from His mouth comes a sharp sword, so that with it He may smite the nations; and he will rule them with a rod of iron; and He treads the wine press of the fierce wrath of God, the Almighty. And on His robe and on His thigh He has a name written, "KING OF KINGS, AND LORD OF LORDS." (Revelation 19:11–16)

Jesus Christ is Lord of all who desire to make their homes an outpost of civilization. One day the Lord Jesus is going to come back to this earth. He's coming to settle up. The Lord Jesus Christ not only rides for the brand; He is the brand. His name is above every name, and His brand is above every brand. To those of us who have been chosen to ride for the brand, and stand for the brand, and fight for the brand, it should be said that of all men, we are most privileged. For it is our honor and our duty to occupy this place until He comes.

Until then, men, stand tall.

WALKING TALL

1. Review Moses' solemn charge in Deuteronomy 6:1–7. Note especially the instructions in verse 7. In Moses' day, families *walked* together to get places. It made for an ideal teaching time as dads could talk about the Lord, the Scriptures, and important issues as they were "on the way." Today's world is more hectic and fast-paced, but the need to "teach your children" is more important than ever. What are some practical ways dads can get alongside their sons and daughters in the course of a normal week? What role could outdoor activities play in this critical responsibility?

2. Moses speaks of teaching our children when we "lie down" and "rise up." How could this work in a typical American household? What are the most likely things that could get in the way of such teaching times? Why is such teaching becoming more and more crucial?

3. How long has it been since you've invited another Christian single, couple, or family into your home to share a meal, to tap into a Bible study, or to watch you burn some hamburgers on the grill? Have you ever had a visiting missionary over for an evening of mutual encouragement? Have you considered hosting a neighborhood evangelistic Bible study in your home? In other words, are your kids getting the idea that your home is an *outpost* for the love and light of Jesus in a world growing darker by the day? What are some other ways you could help your family catch that vision?

Multnomah Publishers
The publisher and author would love to hear your comments about this book. *Please contact us at:*
www.multnomah.net/standingtall

NOTES

1. Louis L'Amour, *Riding for the Brand* (New York: Bantam, 1986), 1.

2. Peggy Noonan, "You'd Cry Too If It Happened to You," *Forbes,* 14 September 1992, 58.

3. Tom Bethell, "Culture War II," *The American Spectator*, July 1993, 16.

4. William J. Bennett, *The Index of Leading Cultural Indicators,* March 1993, vol. 1 (Washington, D.C.: The Heritage Foundation).

5. Paul Harvey as quoted in *Leadership* 8, no. 1 (Winter 1987): 41.

6. Daniel Patrick Moynihan, cited by James Dale Davidson and Lord William Rees-Moog, *The Great Reckoning* (New York: Simon and Schuster, 1993), 291.

7. Phil Gramm, "Don't Let Judges Set Crooks Free," *New York Times,* 8 July 1993, A13.

8. John Leo, "When Cities Give up Their Streets," *U.S. News and World Report,* 26 July 1993, 20.

9. Wess Roberts, *Leadership Secrets of Attila the Hun* (New York: Warner Books, 1985), iv, 2.

10. Charles W. Colson, *Against the Night* (Ann Arbor, Mich.: Servant Books, 1989), 23, 46.

11. Ibid., 39.

12. Allan Bloom, *The Closing of the American Mind* (New York: Simon and Schuster, 1987).

13. Colson, *Against the Night,* 41.

14. Steven Isaac, "Undressed," Plugged In, Focus on the Family, http://www.family.org/pplace/pi/tv, November 2000.

15. Michael Medved, *Hollywood vs. America* (New York: Harper Collins, 1992), 147.

16. Charles R. Swindoll, *You and Your Child* (Nashville, Tenn.: Thomas Nelson Publishers, 1977), 64.

17. T. K. Abbott, cited by Fritz Rienecker, *A Linguistic Key to the Greek New Testament* (Grand Rapids, Mich.: Regency Reference, 1976), 582.

18. *Leadership* 14, no. 4 (Fall 1993): 56. I have taken the liberty of changing some of the details of this story to fit the narrative.

19. Michael Green, source unknown.

20. Ken R. Canfield, *The 7 Secrets of Effective Fathers* (Grand Rapids, Mich.: Zondervan, 1992), 79.

21. Stuart Briscoe, source unknown.

22. Adam Smith, *Paper Money* (New York: Summit Books, 1981), 230.

23. John Eldredge and Greg Jesson, *Community Impact Curriculum,* Focus on the Family, Colorado Springs, 20.

24. David A. Noebel, *Understanding the Times* (Manitou Springs, Colo.: Summit Press, 1989), 622.

25. Cited by David A. Noebel, Richard John Neuhaus, *The Naked Public Square* (Grand Rapids, Mich.: Eerdmans, 1984), 95.

26. Cited by D. James Kennedy, "The Separation of Church and State," *American Family Association Journal* 17, no. 1 (January 1993): 18.

27. David Barton, *The Bulletproof George Washington* (Aledo, Tex.: Wallbuilders Press, 1990).

28. Ibid., back cover.

29. Kennedy, "The Separation," 18.

30. Ibid.

31. Bruce L. Shelley, *Church History in Plain Language* (Waco, Tex.: Word, 1982), 361.

32. Ibid., 334.

33. Francis A. Schaeffer, *The Complete Works of Francis A. Schaeffer: A Christian Worldview, Volume Five, A Christian View of the West* (Westchester, Ill.: Crossway Books, 1982), 139.

34. Eldredge and Jesson, *Community Impact Curriculum*, 21.

35. Edward L. Lederman, "When Students Take Guns into School," *Human Events*, 9 May 1992.

36. Charles Colson, "Clogged Courts Drain the Nation," *Jubilee,* April 1992, 7.

37. Ibid., 7.

38. Eldredge and Jesson, *Community Impact Curriculum,* 7. Also *National and International Religion Report* 5, no. 24 (18 November 1991): 7.

39. Rush Limbaugh, *The Way Things Ought to Be* (New York: Pocket Books, 1992), 299.

40. Ibid., 104.

41. *The Wittenberg Door*, interview with Rush Limbaugh, November 1993.

42. Os Guiness, *The American Hour* (New York: The Free Press, 1993), 180.

43. Gary T. Amos, *Defending the Declaration* (Brentwood, Tenn.: Wolgemuth & Hyatt, 1989), 39.

44. *World Book Encyclopedia,* s.v. "United States Constitution."

45. William Sanford Lasor, David Allan Hubbard, and Frederic William Bush, *Old Testament Survey* (Grand Rapids, Mich.: Eerdmans Publishing, 1982), 266.

46. Leon Wood, *A Survey of Israel's History,* 310.

47. James Edward Anderson, "The Idolatrous Worship of Baal by Israel," (Ph.D. diss., Dallas Theological Seminary, 1975), 396.

48. Gayle Reaves, "Abortion Rights Backers, Foes Re-Examining Tactics," *Dallas Morning News,* 28 June 1993, 1A.

49. Albert Gore, *Earth in the Balance* (New York: The Penguin Group, 1993), 23.

50. John Aaron Flack, "The Influence of Canaanite Civilization on the Children of Israel," (master's thesis, Dallas Theological Seminary, 1958), 11.

51. Charles Swindoll, *The Life and Times of Elijah* (Anaheim, Calif.: Insight for Living, 1992), 4.

52. J. Oswald Sanders, *Robust in Faith* (Chicago: Moody Press, 1965), 125.

53. Gore, *Earth in the Balance,* 119.

54. Ibid.

55. Chuck and Donna McIlhenny, *When the Wicked Seize a City* (Lafayette, La: Huntington House, 1993), 40.

56. Roger J. Magnuson, *Are Gay Rights Right?* (Portland, Ore.: Multnomah Press, 1990), 15.

57. McIlhenny, *When the Wicked Seize a City,* 126.

58. Ibid., 127.

59. Ibid., 18.

60. Cited by George Grant and Mark A. Horne, *Legislating Immorality* (Chicago: Moody, 1993), 33.

61. Matthys Levy and Mario Salvadori, *Why Buildings Fall Down* (New York: W. W. Norton & Company, 1992), 221.

62. Anderson, "The Idolatrous Worship of Baal by Israel," 159.

63. McIlhenny, *When the Wicked Seize a City,* 78.

64. Ibid., 212.

65. Magnuson, *Are Gay Rights Right?,* 31.

66. Robert H. Knight, "Homosexuality Is Not a Civil Right" (Washington D.C.: Family Research Council in Focus).

67. Magnuson, *Are Gay Rights Right?*

68. Knight, "Homosexuality Is Not a Civil Right," 4.

69. Grant, *Legislating Immorality,* 67.

70. Grant, *Legislating Immorality,* 43.

71. Dr. Paul Cameron, "Child Molestation and Homosexuality," Family Research Institute, 3.

72. Ibid., 4.

73. Ibid., 5–6.

74. Grant, *Legislating Immorality,* 42.

75. Magnuson, *Are Gay Rights Right?,* 13.

76. Ibid., 14.

77. Robert H. Knight, "Flawed Science Nurtures Genetic Origin for Homosexuality," Family Research Council in Focus.

78. Ibid., 1.

79. Grant, *Legislating Immorality,* 170. (Author's note: I am indebted to George Grant for supplying this information on homosexual groups.)

80. Ibid., 197.

81. *Christianity Today,* "Homosexual Debate Strains Campus Harmony," 22 November 1993, 38.

82. Stanton L. Jones, "The Loving Opposition: Speaking the Truth in a Climate of Hate," *Christianity Today,* 19 July 1993, 24.

83. Ibid., 20

84. Ibid.

85. Lewis Smedes, *Sex for Christians* (Grand Rapids, Mich.: William B. Eerdmans, 1976), 72.

86. Cited by Trudy Hutchens, "Homosexuality: Born or Bred?" *Family Voice,* Concerned Women of America, June 1993.

87. Joseph Nicolosi, Ph.D., *Reparative Therapy of Male Homosexuality* (Northvale, N.J.: Jason Aronson, 1991), inside cover flap.

88. *Dallas Morning News,* 27 June 1993, 1A.

89. "For the Love of Kids: What Should Be Done with a Teacher Who Belongs to a Pedophile Group but Has a Spotless Record?" *Time,* 1 November 1993, 51.

90. Ibid.

91. "100 Minutes to Freedom," *People,* 11 January 1993, 52.

92. J. Oswald Sanders, *Robust in Faith* (Chicago, Ill.: Moody Press, 1965), 126.

93. Matthew Henry, *Commentary on the Whole Bible* (Grand Rapids, Mich.: Zondervan Publishing House, Regency Reference Library, 1961), 385.

94. J. Vernon McGee, *Through the Bible,* Vol. 2 (Nashville, Tenn.: Thomas Nelson Publishers, 1982), 282.

95. Ibid.

96. Cited in *Leadership* 4, no. 2 (Spring 1983): 93.

97. Warren W. Wiersbe, *Wiersbe's Expository Outlines on the Old Testament* (Wheaton, Ill.: Victor Books, 1993), 318.

98. Wilson L. Harrell, "Facing Fire: Combat Creates Entrepreneurial Leaders," *Success* 40, no. 1 (February 1993): 9.

99. John Gardner, *On Leadership* (New York: The Free Press, 1990), 169.

100. Oswald Chambers, source unknown.

101. John Luther, source unknown.

102. Roger von Oech, *A Whack on the Side of the Head* (New York: Warner Books, 1983), 6.

103. Ibid., 25.

104. Gardner, *On Leadership,* 2.

105. Ibid., 4.

106. David R. Johnson, *The Light behind the Star* (Sisters, Ore.: Questar Publishers, 1989), 93–6.

107. Tom Clancy, *Submarine: A Guided Tour Inside a Nuclear Warship* (New York: Berkley Books, 1993), xix.

108. Ross Campbell, *How to Really Love Your Child* (Wheaton, Ill.: Victor Books, 1984).

109. Chuck Colson, "The Human Animal," *Breakpoint,* 10 August 1993, no. 30810.

110. Cited by Warren Bennis, *On Becoming a Leader* (New York: Addison Wesley Publishing, 1989), 197.

111. *Leadership* 8, no. 3 (Summer 1992): 47.

112. *Leadership* 14, no. 1 (Winter 1993): 49.

113. Colson, *Against the Night.*

114. Karyn Henley, *The Beginner's Bible* (Grand Rapids, Mich.: Zondervan Publishing Houses, 1997).

115. Mack Thomas, *The Wonder Bible* (Sisters, Ore.: Questar Publishers, 1993).

116. Allan Bloom, *The Closing of the American Mind* (New York: Simon and Schuster, 1987).

117. "Grandpa (Tell Me 'Bout the Good Old Days)," The Judds, ©1986, RCA.

118. Cited by Anderson, "The Idolatrous Worship," 355.

STEVE FARRAR
IN PERSON—IN YOUR CITY

STEVE FARRAR'S
Men's Leadership Conference

Thousands of men have discovered
that, as in the pages of his books,
Steve Farrar also shoots straight in
person. His Men's Leadership
Conferences are held all across America
to equip men to be better husbands,
better fathers, better grandfathers, and
more effective spiritual leaders.

CONFERENCE TOPICS:

- How to Be a Godly Leader

- How to Discern the
  Culture Today

- How to Spiritually Lead
  Your Family

- How to Be a Godly Husband

- How to Raise Masculine Sons
  and Feminine Daughters

- How to Be a Godly Father
  and Grandfather

- How to Finish Strong
  in the Christian Life

"Steve Farrar is right on target,
he understands our times,
he talks straight, he doesn't mess around,
and best of all, he walks the talk!"
CHUCK SWINDOLL
PRESIDENT, DALLAS THEOLOGICAL SEMINARY
RADIO SPEAKER, "INSIGHT FOR LIVING"

For more information
about attending or hosting
a conference, call

1-800-MEN-LEAD

Solid Leadership Strategies from the Greatest Commander of All

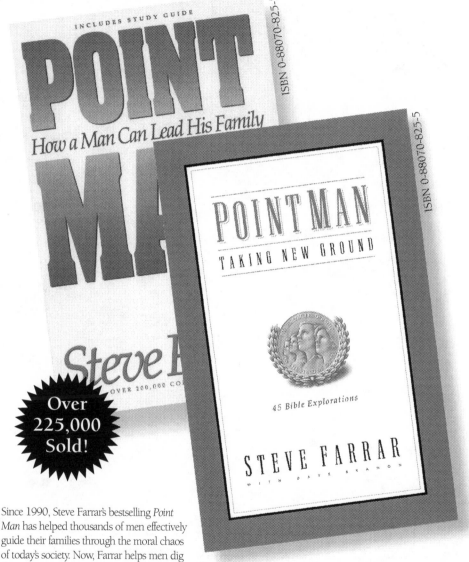

ISBN 0-88070-825-5

ISBN 0-88070-825-5

Over 225,000 Sold!

Since 1990, Steve Farrar's bestselling *Point Man* has helped thousands of men effectively guide their families through the moral chaos of today's society. Now, Farrar helps men dig deeper into God's Word for solid, biblical direction to help them meet this goal.

Building upon the crucial topics introduced in *Point Man*, Farrar's *Point Man: Taking New Ground* explores God's teachings about the subjects most important to husbands and fathers today. Each of these forty-five easy-to-complete readings includes:

- Daily Scripture and devotional passages
- Key Bible verses
- Practical, personal applications
- Daily prayers, and more!

INCLUDES STUDY GUIDE

POINT
How a Man Can Lead His Family
MAN

Steve F

OVER 200,000 CO

POINT MAN
TAKING NEW GROUND

45 Bible Explorations

STEVE FARRAR
WITH DAVE BRANON

"Run so that you may obtain the prize."
1 Corinthians 9:24

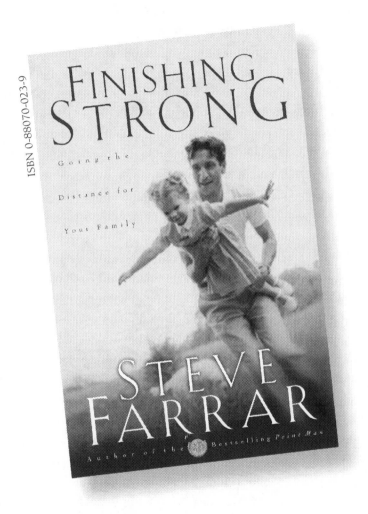

ISBN 0-88070-023-9

Every day, men see husbands and fathers around them falling to temptations such as workaholism, infidelity, uncontrolled anger, and ethical shortcuts. No man wants to hurt his wife and children. But if he is to "finish strong," living righteously and ethically to the end of his life, he must proactively implement the commitments he has made to Jesus Christ and to his family. In *Finishing Strong*, bestselling men's author Steve Farrar shows husbands and dads how they can do exactly that, teaching them how to recognize and avoid the pitfalls that can destroy a family and inspiring them to live with character and conviction.

Printed in the United States
by Baker & Taylor Publisher Services